Conspiracy &

Eirikur Bergmann

Conspiracy & Populism

The Politics of Misinformation

palgrave
macmillan

Eirikur Bergmann
Centre for European Studies
Bifröst University
Borgarbyggd, Iceland

ISBN 978-3-319-90358-3   ISBN 978-3-319-90359-0   (eBook)
https://doi.org/10.1007/978-3-319-90359-0

Library of Congress Control Number: 2018939717

This Palgrave Macmillan imprint is published by the registered company Springer Nature
Switzerland AG
The registered company address is: Gewerbestrasse 11, 6330 Cham, Switzerland

This book is dedicated to my partner in life,
Aino Freyja Järvelä.

Preface and Acknowledgements

It was a beautiful, clear summer day in 2011. The sun was shining bright where I was standing out on the deck of a ferry, sailing with a group of family and friends to the small island of *Flatey*, just off the western coast of Iceland. Soon, I started noticing my fellow passengers becoming preoccupied with their phones, their faces turning whiter. I dug out my device and rapidly realised that something serious was happening in Norway, on the small island of Utøya, perhaps a not so different isle to the one I was heading to—and, actually, not very far from where I once myself lived in Norway. The reception on my phone was poor, and the reports weren't all that clear. Still, it seemed evident that someone was massacring young members of the Norwegian Labour party.

Over the coming hours, we learned the full details of this horrible terrorist attack. I opened the so-called manifesto of the attacker, Anders Behring Breivik, and read of his fears of those he referred to as cultural Marxists, evil multiculturalists that he accused of ruining his home country in an ongoing devious plot of turning Norway into an Islamist society. The document was filled with many more of the most commonly upheld conspiracy theories of the far-right in the West.

Just a few years later, the murderer of British Labour Party MP, Jo Cox, justified his crime with that same rhetoric.

During the Brexit campaign in the UK, Vote Leave argued that because of the high birth rate in Turkey, one million Muslim Turks would soon be arriving in the UK. When criticised by many specialists for unfounded claims, a leading Brexit campaigner replied saying: 'I think the people in this country have had enough of experts.'

Timothy McVeigh, who blew up the Oklahoma federal building in 1995, had been convinced that the US government was plotting a dictatorial communist New World Order. Many of his mates further insisted that Nazi extermination camps never existed, that they were a hoax.

In the Netherlands, the leader of the Freedom Party, Geert Wilders, insisted that the Dutch people were being replaced by foreign infiltrators. In France, Marine Le Pen of the National Front maintained that Europe was being invaded by hordes of 'stinking' dark-skinned migrants and 'rat people' flowing in a 'river of sperm.' In America, President Donald Trump wrote this when justifying banning people from several Muslim dominated countries from entering the US: 'I think Islam hates us.'

Over in Russia, the Kremlin insisted that members of the protest punk band, Pussy Riot, were agents in a Western led conspiracy of emasculating the Russian state.

These were some of the events and statements—all discussed and referenced in this book—that got me thinking about the impact of far-right populist conspiracy theories (CTs). My previous research into Nordic nationalism and the rise of right-wing populists in Europe also pushed me onto the path of investigating CTs upheld in their politics, which is the subject of this book.

This research has benefitted from interaction with many colleagues in several academic fields. Two Europe wide academic networks have been especially useful. Participating in the EU funded COST action, *Populist Political Communication in Europe,* provided me with valuable access to much of the most recent research on European populism. And involvement in the EU funded COST action, *Comparative Analysis of Conspiracy Theories* (*COMPACT*), exposed me to some of the most pristine studies of CTs. I believe my engagement in these networks, and several other inter-disciplinary collaborations, place me in a favourable position to examine and compare the two tropes of study in this book.

I thank my colleagues in these projects for their fruitful cooperation. I thank my publishers at Palgrave Macmillan, Ambra Finotello and Imogen Gordon Clark, for their flawless cooperation, and for all their valuable help.

This book is dedicated to my partner in life, Aino Freyja Järvelä. I thank her and our four children, Sólrún Rós, Einar Sigurður, Hrafnhildur and Ægir—who all keep wondering about the world and continuously question its politics—for their patience and support, and not least, for stimulating discussions throughout the writing process.

Madrid, Spain   Eirikur Bergmann

Contents

Abbreviations

AfD	Alternative for Germany (*Alternative für Deutschland*)
BBC	British Broadcasting Company
BNP	British National Party
Brexit	Exit of Britain from the European Union
CDA	Critical Discourse Analysis
CIA	Central Intelligence Agency of the United States
CTs	Conspiracy Theories
DF	Danish Peoples Party, (*Dansk Folkeparti*)
EP	European Parliament
EU	European Union
FEMA	Federal Emergency Management Agency of the United States
FN	Front National in France
FPÖ	Freedom Party of Austria, (*Freiheitliche Partei Österreichs*)
FRP	Progress Party of Denmark, (*Fremskridtspartiet*); Progress Party of Norway, (*Fremskrittspartiet*)
FT	The Financial Times
IMF	International Monetary Fund
ISIS	Islamic State, Terrorist Organization
JFK	John F. Kennedy
KZB	Khazarian Zionist Bolshevik
MEP	Member of European Parliament

MP   Member of Parliament
NAFTA   North America Free Trade Agreement
NATO   North Atlantic Treaty Organization
NHS   National Health Service of the UK
NSA   National Security Agency of the United States
OEEC   Organization for Economic Cooperation in Europe
PS   Finns Party, True Finns, (*Perussuomalaiset*)
RT   Russia Today, TV station
SD   Sweden Democrats (*Sverigedemokraterna*)
UFO   Unknown Foreign Object
UKIP   UK Independence Party
UN   United Nations
WB   World Bank
WHO   World Health Organization
WWI   First World War
WWII   Second World War
ZOG   Zionist Occupation Government

1

Introduction

In the morning of Friday 22. July 2011, a 32-year-old resident of a farmhouse in Hedemark near Oslo packed his van and drove into the city. After being held up in final preparations, he parked his van in front of the office of the Prime Minister in the middle of the administration area. Setting his plan in motion, he detonated a bomb, killing 8 people. From the governmental quarter in Oslo, Anders Behring Breivik, a native Norwegian, travelled to Utøya Island, located in Tyrilfjorden, 38 kilometres west of the capital city, where Norway's Labour Party youth movement held its annual summer gathering. There he slaughtered 69 people with an assault rifle, most of the victims were very young members of the party.

This was the most horrible incident of Nordic extreme nationalism in contemporary times. Seventy-seven people died in the terrorist attack. Before leaving his farmhouse in the morning, Breivik (2011) had published a 1500 page-long document online titled *2083: A European Declaration of Independence*. He had distributed it via e-mail to several people around the world that he thought were of like mind to his. In this lengthy document—a rather incoherent compendium of writings he had pasted together from several sites online and then scattered his own

© The Author(s) 2018
E. Bergmann, *Conspiracy & Populism*, https://doi.org/10.1007/978-3-319-90359-0_1

thoughts in between other people's texts—he argued that Europe was being ruined by the influx of Muslim immigrants, that the continent was culturally under siege by foreign infiltrators. He went on to accuse mainly feminists and the social democratic elite of having betrayed the European public into the hands of their external enemies, presumably, he argued, in order to implement their malignant ideology of multiculturalism. With his act, Breivik wanted to prevent a cultural suicide of Europe, underway and orchestrated by those he described as cultural Marxists. He called for the deportation of all Muslims from Europe.

Anders Breivik was a believer in the so-called *Eurabia* conspiracy theory (CT), more precisely, he maintained that the European Union (EU) was a project to culturally turn the continent into Eurabia—the insistence that Muslims, with the support of domestic elites in Europe, were plotting to turn the continent into an Islamic society. Breivik considered himself being a Christian knight, dedicated to stemming the tide of Muslim migration into Europe. In the manifesto, he accused his victims in the Norwegian Labour Party of being responsible for ruining his country's Nordic heritage with their feminist and multicultural beliefs.

Breivik was a lone wolf attacker. Still, he claimed to belong to the international Christian organization of the Knight Templar, fighting a holy war against Marxism and multiculturalism. Apparently, though, he seemed to have been the only official and active member, at least of his faction.

Previously, Breivik had belonged to the Norwegian populist Progress Party, which he later found to be too soft on immigration. He then plugged into a loose-knit underground network of militants, mostly communicating their racist message below the surface online. His terrorist attack revealed a hidden subculture in Norway, simmering undetected on the Internet. This was a network of racist and Islamophobic groups, scattered around the country. One of the main forums for this sort of politics, was the online platform document.no, where Norwegian racists exchanged their views. Breivik's main hero on the platform was a Norwegian anti-Muslim blogger, who called himself Fjordman. This 'dark prophet of Norway'—as he was referred to—predicted that ethnic Norwegians would soon be in minority if the political elite was allowed to continue destroying European culture and turn the continent into a Eurabia (see Bergmann 2017).

Breivik's atrocity was a response to a call that Fjordman and others within the network had issued: a moral call aimed at all cultural conservatives to defy the demographic infiltration of Muslims; a quest in which all Muslims would be expelled from Norway (Seierstad 2015).

Perfectly in line with what both populists and conspiracy theorists have in common—as will be examined at length in this book—he also accused the internal elite of betraying the domestic public into the hands of the external threat. He then turned to designate himself as the true defender of the public, taking on the malignant forces.

In August 2012, Breivik was convicted of mass murder, for causing a fatal explosion, and for terrorism. He was sentenced to 21 years in prison. The ruling included a clause of preventive detention, meaning that his incarceration could be prolonged as long as he was deemed a threat to society.

This horrible terrorist attack in Norway was just one example of the effects that extreme right-wing conspiracy theorists can have on unstable recipients of their messages. It seems that Anders Breivik genuinely believed that with his actions, he was coming to the defence of European culture, which was under attack from Muslims, who in a systemic way—and with help of domestic traitors—were plotting to conquer Europe and dispose of the European culture.

In this book, I examine the link between CTs and right-wing populism. More precisely, I analyse how right-wing populists apply CTs to advance their politics and support for their parties.

Rise of Populist Conspiracy Theories

The rapid rise of right-wing populist political parties around Europe and across the Atlantic in the early new millennium, coincided with the simultaneous increased spread of CTs. The two phenomena are intertwined, as is explored in this book. Still, not all populists are conspiracy theorists and CTs don't necessarily all have a populist political side. However, right-wing populists have proved to be especially prone to create and promote CTs, which is investigated here.

In his novel, *Running Dog*, Don DeLillo (1978) wrote of the 'age of conspiracy' in American politics. Now, it seems, we are experiencing the age of the populists, who in their politics have fully embraced CTs. The merger of the two was perhaps most obviously personified in US President Donald Trump. In their discourse analysis of campaign speeches, Eric Oliver and Wendy Rahn (2016) found that in the 2016 presidential election, Trump was far more frequently and more extensively than any other candidate prone to apply 'rhetoric that is distinctive in its simplicity, anti-elitism and collectivism.' This seemed to sit well with his core voter base, as in the same study they were found to also be distinctive in their nativism and their 'high-level of conspiratorial thinking.' Oliver and Rahn concluded that those in their study that held anti-elite sentiments and were mistrusting of experts, correlated highly on the conspiratorial scale. Those who saw the system as being stacked against them, were 'far more likely to endorse CTs of all types.'

Classical CTs of the radical-right tended, initially, to revolve around anti-Semitic sentiments, often involving ideas of a Zionist plot of taking over control in the world. Or of a wider New World Order conspiracy, led by, for example, Marxists and feminists, aiming at ending the Western dominated capitalist order. Many radical-right parties started out fighting a communist conspiracy, but have since moved on to unravel a globalist covert conspiracy, led by a band of domestic liberals and international actors, for example, within cross-border organizations such as the EU, the United Nations (UN) and the International Monetary Fund (IMF). Another common theme was identifying and uprooting what is referred to as the deep-state, the idea of a covert network of bureaucrats, professional politicians and interest agencies controlling society behind the scenes.

In recent years, nationalist right-wing populists in Europe and in America have firmly turned their sights on Muslim migrants, with a rapid proliferation of CTs revolving around *Islamification* of the West, for example, of Sharia laws being instated in Europe and in the USA. In many such cases, Muslim immigrants were portrayed as invaders, often seen as soldiers in a coordinated cultural and religious quest of conquering Europe.

In History and All Around

According to common caricature, conspiracy theorists are often depicted as being marginalised conservative middle-aged white males. However, as will be documented here, conspiracy thinking is much more widespread than that. People of all ethnicities, social and economic classes, ages, political inclinations, and across territories, believe in CTs. Still, social and cultural differences can predict which CTs they might believe, and, in some cases, indicate their level of conspiratorialism.

In history, many societies have been infested with CTs. In the wake of the Great Fire of Rome in CE 64, for example, rumours were immediately blazing of Emperor Nero, himself, setting fire to his own city (Brotherton 2015). Polities based on authoritative governance have been especially prone to subscribe to them. Hitler's Germany and Stalin's Russia were, for instance, infested with vast and far-reaching CTs. In his book, *Ur-Fascism*, Italian writer Umberto Eco (1995), who was born in Mussolini's fascist Italy, wrote about fascists' reliance on CTs. He said that fascism could come back under the most innocent of guises. 'Our duty is to uncover it and to point our finger at any of its new instances—every day, in every part of the world.' In fascism, he wrote, individuals have no rights. Instead, 'the People is conceived as a quality, a monolithic entity expressing the Common Will.' Eco said that since large groups of people don't usually share a common will, the leader becomes their interpreter. 'The People is only a theatrical fiction,' he wrote. 'We no longer need the Piazza Venezia in Rome or the Nuremberg Stadium. There is in our future a TV or Internet populism, in which the emotional response of a selected group of citizens can be presented and accepted as the Voice of the People.'

In the 1920s and 1930s, several European democracies fell into authoritarianism—fascism on the political right and communism on the political left. Yale Professor, Timothy Snyder (2017), argues that both versions were, of sorts, a response to the globalisation of the time, which was seen as a conspiracy against the nation. The current trend of nationalist right-wing populism examined here is also squarely anti-globalist. It is, thus, not unimaginable that ideas leading to similar fascist tendencies can—as Eco warned against—creep back into modern western democracies.

Fascist regimes are, though, only one example of societies infested with CTs. Another, and of a completely different kind was, for instance, found amongst the African tribe of the Azande, who believed in witchcraft. As Edvard Evans-Pritchard (1937) documented, the Azande people didn't believe in coincidences at all and explained most misfortune by result of witchcraft. Conspiracy theories are here, thus, also related to rumours, urban legends, folklore, mythology and fairy tales. These are unproven stories told as truths.

Conspiratorialism is also widespread in many contemporary societies, such as around the Arab world, where there is even a cultural disposition to conspiratorial thinking.

Stigma

Conspiracy theories have not always been viewed as negative, and in some places of the world they might, indeed, still not be seen as entirely deleterious, but perhaps rather as a sensible view of the world. The same applies to populism, which in several instances has been celebrated by both leaders and followers. Still, neither *populism* nor *conspiracy theory* are neutral analytical terms in contemporary political discourse in the western world. Rather, these are pejorative markers similar to extremism, terrorism and other negative labels.

Commonly, people don't refer to themselves as being a populist or a conspiracy theorist. These are tags applied to others who are not deemed rational, terms used to discredit their politics or alternative explanations of events, which is treated as stigmatised knowledge. Conspiracy theorists are thus often dismissed as offering bogus explanations and accused of dangerous politics or world-views. In other words, these are exclusionary and alienating concepts applied when ridiculing others who are not accepted into the mainstream. Thus, as these are often terms used to belittle or marginalise rival explanations, the examiner must be careful when applying them to his subjects.

Links to Extremism

Several incidents and occurrences can be identified that have led many people to question the sincerity of the West, including, for instance, aspects regarding the invasion of Iraq in 2003, the financial crisis of 2008, and the migration crisis that heightened in 2015 in the wake of the conflict in Syria. Some of those individuals that began to question authorities on these kinds of key issues have also started to believe in CT's. This can be a cause for concern, for when suspecting authorities of deception, people might also not be as inclined to follow their guidance in other areas, such as health and protection.

This is furthermore significant, for example, as studies have found CTs to be a catalyst for extremism (van Prooijen et al. 2015). Indeed, many of the most influential scholars of CTs (e.g. Hofstadter 1964; Pipes 1999; Byford 2011; Popper 2012; Barkun 2013) have tended to treat conspiracy theorists as violent and dangerous extremists who are a threat to the world order. Conspiracy theories are blamed for some of the worst acts in world history, bringing with them war and destruction. Their promoters have included some of the world's most notorious leaders. In addition to Hitler and Stalin already mentioned, we can add, for instance, Benito Mussolini, Pol Pot, Idi Amin and Saddam Hussein. Jovan Byford (2011) concludes that CTs 'remain the refuge of every dictator and authoritarian leader in the world.'

Most of the scholars mentioned above agree that CTs can fuel aggression and polarization in society. Byford (2011) argues that 'conspiracism has been a stable ingredient of discrimination, antidemocratic and populist politics.' He thus maintains that CTs have led to 'violence,' 'totalitarianism' and 'mass-murders.'

In other words, CTs can pose a serious threat to democratic societies.

Moving into the Mainstream

As explored here, CT's are, no longer—if they ever were—a phenomena found primarily on the fringes of society. For instance, as will be documented in this book, more than half of Americans don't believe the official version of the John F. Kennedy assassination, that the President was killed by Lee Harvey Oswald acting alone. In the UK, a significant number of people don't buy the official explanation surrounding the death of Princess Diana. Around a third of US citizens think global warming is a hoax. Between 30 and 40% of the US population does not believe official accounts of the 9/11 attacks. In other words, a third of them suspect the government of either covering up real accounts of horrendous events or even of being in on it themselves. These examples indicate that in making sense of the world, many people treat alternative tales as equally plausible to official accounts. Nowadays, there are not many major events in the word, such as outbreaks of military conflict, plane crashes, natural disasters, large scale public protests or political assassinations, that don't attract significant CTs around them.

Populism has gone mainstream as well. The rise of populists around Europe and in the USA indicates that the phenomena is no longer isolated on the fringes. Rather, we have entered the era of the populist—the conspiratorial populist. This has led to the emergence of what has been branded *Post-Truth* politics, where the overflow of information drowns out facts and public discourse appeals rather to emotions and personal belief.

As will be investigated here, both CTs and populism are, thus, deeply integrated into contemporary democratic politics. They are no longer only the tools of powerless protestors and no longer merely a symptom of a crisis of democracy, rather these elements are being firmly woven into democratic societies.

However, despite being widespread, that does not in itself mitigate the threat that CTs can pose in and to society. On the contrary, experiments discussed in this book have shown that being exposed to CTs decreases trust in government institutions. Thus, the increased spread of CTs can undermine democracy and social trust.

In scholarly work, as well as in media reporting, the most attention to both populists and conspiracy theorists has been given to those on the margins of western societies, in other words, to relatively powerless actors who challenge the mainstream political order from the fringe. As a result, another strand of nationalist right-wing populist CTs has been somewhat overlooked, that is, the rapid proliferation of CTs spread from within the very power centres themselves, for example, by several contemporary authoritarian political leaders.

In Russia, President Vladimir Putin, for instance, long upheld claims of the West actively plotting in secret to bring down the Russian state. And in America, President Donald Trump has, amongst many other novel discursive creations, branded the media as being enemies of the people, claiming that the mainstream media was systematically producing and broadcasting false stories that were specifically aimed to harm the American people. Another example is when without any evidence, he claimed that thousands of Muslims in New Jersey had celebrated the 9/11 attacks.

Many of the CTs discussed in this book might be viewed as merely amusing tales, were it not for those people that take them seriously enough to cause harm to others.

Multi-disciplinary

Conspiracy theories usually derive from a social political or psychological origin. Still, as established here, they are of diverse kinds and can be classified according to different criteria. CTs are also understood in variety of ways. It is therefore perhaps not surprising that the phenomenon has been subject of study across many different academic disciplines, with scholars from various fields analysing them from diverse viewpoints. Most prominent have been students of social science, literature, culture, philosophy, history, psychology, media and political science. Many of these scholars remain true to their own discipline and thus reach quite different kinds of conclusions, while others take a transdisciplinary approach (see further in Butter and Knight 2016).

Philosopher Karl Popper was one of the first scholars to open up the debate on CTs. He was concerned that their spread could bring on a totalitarian regime. In his influential book, *The Open Society and Its Enemies*, published in 1945, he wrote of the 'conspiracy theory of society,' the claim that all results, even those which at first sight do not seem to be intended by anyone, are still the anticipated result of the actions of people who are interested in these results. Firmly believing that societies should be examined as unintended consequences of complex actions, Popper viewed CTs to be the opposite of what he deemed was the true aim of social science.

It is generally accepted that contemporary academic studies into CTs date back to the publication of historian Richard Hofstadter's (1964) essay, *The Paranoid Style in American Politics*. Hofstadter saw conspiracy theorists as harmful deviants, delusional people who by undermining necessary trust in public institutions were ripping apart the fabric of our societies.

As CTs have historically proven to be a quite persistent feature in American society, it is perhaps not surprising that Americanist scholars were amongst the first to investigate the phenomenon. Many scholars have demonstrated how Americans have tended to be especially suspicious of government authority (Oliver and Wood 2014). Some have referred to a conspiracy mania spreading in America. Scholarly work in the field has thus often focused on the American versions.

The conspiracy theory concept, as a practical political term, is relatively young in the USA. Lance de Haven-Smith (2014) illustrates how it was in the 1960s used by the US Central Intelligence Agency (CIA) to discredit conspiracy theories about the death of John F. Kennedy.

Conspiratorialism has featured prominently in American culture. The so-called Red Scare in the USA in the wake of the Second World War, when many feared a communist infiltration, spurred an avalanche of conspiratorial Cold War literature. Of course, secret plots have for a long time and in many places, been popular in literature. One obvious example is Shakespeare's *Hamlet*. However, these themes have been especially persistent in contemporary American literature, for instance, in Dan Brown's popular novels. Conspiratorialism has also filtered easily into movies and television shows. Blockbuster conspiratorial movies include for example: *The Bourne Identity* and *Mission Impossible* sequels, the films: *Conspiracy Theory, Enemy of the State, The Firm, JFK, The Manchurian Candidate* and *Wag the Dog*. Amongst the most popular television series were the *X-files* in the 1990s, which was accompanied with the mantra 'Trust No One.' More recently, the Netflix series *House of Cards* is another example.

This trend has led to growing interest amongst scholars of literature to explore the phenomenon. Many of them have examined CTs as a specific narrative in its own right. Conspiracy theories tend to uncover dramatic plots and revolve around both protagonists and antagonists, the fight between the good hero and evil villain. In general, CTs usually include a story of a dramatic event, usually a powerful villain (the conspirators) and heroes (the whistle blower). As a common narrative, CTs attempt to provide a coherent view of events or of the social order. They tell a story of the present state of affairs and provide a reason for them. Most often, these are fascinating tales of demonic enemies plotting against the common good and the brave quest of the heroic but powerless whistle-blower who is struggling on behalf of the ordinary man in the good fight against their oppressors.

In addition to cultural studies scholars, conspiratorialism has also long been a subject of study within the field of social psychology. Generally, social psychologists have tended to view CTs as some sort of deviation. Often, they are mostly concerned with the harmful effects of belief in CTs. Therefore, their focus has often been by way of experiments and surveys on investigating cognitive biases and attempting to discover what causes conspiracy beliefs. Social psychologists thus tend to treat conspiracy theorists as dangerous out-groups.

Sociology, as a field of study and CTs, as such, unite in an effort to make sense of the social order and attempt to explain the reality. It is thus not surprising that CTs have long been a keen interest within the field of sociology studies. With CTs moving faster into the political arena, political scientists have also taken a growing interest in the phenomena, especially accompanying the rapid rise of populist political parties, who have proved to be prone to apply CTs in their political rhetoric. Most recently, with fake news hitting the western world like a tsunami, media scholars have also become more involved in the field.

As will be discussed here, populism has also been studied from an array of different approaches, such as political science, communication studies, historical analysis, social psychology, political economy and democratic theory.

Definitions and Concepts

The multi-disciplinary nature of the research already conducted into CTs has produced a variety of definitions useful in framing the phenomena. This book aims to investigate the intersection of these two relatively young scholarly strands, populism studies and the field conspiracy theory studies, which are too often examined separately. Although the focus here is primarily on right-wing populists, CTs upheld by other kinds of populists will also be discussed when appropriate for context.

For the purpose of this book, definitions of specifically nationalist right-wing populists are framed through identifying a threefold claim for their support of *the people*. First, they tend discursively to create an external threat to the nation. Secondly, they accuse the domestic elite of betraying the people, often of even siding with external forces. Thirdly, they position themselves as the only true defenders of the pure people they vow to protect against these malignant outsiders, that is; against those that they themselves have discursively created. These features, further discussed in later chapters, may help in identifying the links in the literature between populism and CTs.

When defining CTs, then, most obviously, they tend to articulate a critique of powerful institutions and depart from progressive analysis by substituting a simplistic populist vision of antagonism between *the people* and *the elites* in place of a detailed analysis of complex power structures.

Both right-ring populists and CTs unite in a *Manichean* world-view, in which societies are seen as divided between *evil elites* who are in control of the *pure people*. According to this binary viewpoint, the pure people are unaware of the malignant parasitic forces exploiting not only their naivety but also their inherited goodness.

When analysing populism and CTs, however, the boundary between CTs, lies and political propaganda can become blurry. It is thus important to separate CTs from rumours, folklore and urban legends.

Furthermore, when a critical account of events and the exercise of tracing probable structures eschewed in favour of, for example the rich and the powerful, moves away from plausibility into becoming a CT, is not always clear. Here, it is important to distinguish, for instance, between critical theory, such as Marxism, from what constitutes a proper CT.

History contains many instances of far-fetched conspiracy theories later proven to be true. One example is of western governments keeping massive surveillance data on ordinary citizens. After having been generally dismissed in the mainstream media as merely a CT, this was later revealed in the 2013 Edward Snowden leak, revealing massive government surveillance projects of the US National Security Agency (NSA) and a British government programme called Tempora (MacAskill et al. 2013).

Theories of conspiracy can, thus, either be right or wrong. They can be reasonable or unreasonable. In this book, we are dealing with those that are, at the time, deemed not credible. In this regard, CTs are rival explanations that according to existing evidence, move away from a plausible account of events.

Aim and Frame

Conspiracy theories have come to function as a form of populist discourse. This book examines CTs within extremists group. The main aim is to investigate the relationship between populism and CTs and frame how particularly right-wing populists, primarily in the Western world, use CT's to advance their politics. The book's principal scholarly contribution is in exploring common tropes of both strands in the literature, and in doing so, identifying the nature of specific populist political CT's, particularly those within the flora of right-wing populist politics. The book will map the process of mainstreamization of both CTs and populist politics, who have, in recent years, moved in from the fringes to feature as a prominent component of contemporary politics across the western world. Another contribution is in analysing the rapid proliferation of CTs spread from within the very power centres.

The exploration in this book draws on critical discourse analysis (CDA), the exersise of identifying the production of ideologies in public discourse. In the understanding of Ruth Wodak (1995), CDA is useful in finding 'structural relationships of dominance, discrimination and control as manifested in language.'

In addition to exploring how CTs and populism intersects and identifying the nature of specifically right-wing populist CTs, by combining the literature of the two separate academic strands, I also specifically explore the CT of an ongoing Islamist takeover of Europe, for example, upheld by Anders Behring Breivik, as discussed at the beginning of this introduction chapter. I examine the rhetoric of many populist political leaders in Europe, into what can be called the Eurabia doctrine. Lastly, I analyse the relationship between CTs and fake news, and how the Internet and social media have led to the proliferation and faster spread of both.

Structure of the Book

In addition to this introduction and concluding remarks, this book consists of five thematic chapters.

In Chapter 2, I start by mapping different kinds of CTs. They are of various kinds and sorts and can be categorized in many different ways. I provide a short general overview of some of the most common CTs upheld in the public domain. The chapter opens with a general introduction into New World Order theories, the unravelling of sinister plots of evil actors controlling the world. Then, I move on to discussing theories of the Antichrist before delving into the many versions of stories surrounding the notorious Illuminati. Next, I discuss anti-religion CTs—anti-Semitic, anti-Catholic and anti-Muslim. Then, I turn to stories around the Bilderberg group and suspicions of deep state actors. Tales around assassinations, false flag operations, deceptions, sinister sciences and politics are next in line, as well as stories around both black and white genocide. Finally, I turn to ranking main CTs.

In Chapter 3, I explore the literature of CT studies and attempt to frame how they might be understood in the context of populist politics. I start with distinguishing between conspiracies and CTs and attempt to define what they constitute. A CT is not a neutral term, rather the label entails stigma. Thus, it is important to compartmentalize them properly and understand both their paranoia and, indeed, also their potential practicalities. Next, I turn to distinguishing between different types of CTs. I explore their internal design and try to understand their nature as non-falsifiable truths and their reliance on both secrecy and agency and how they tend to make a distinction between good and evil in making sense of the world. Then, I turn to identifying the people who might believe in CTs. I discuss their appeal and investigate what causes people to turn to conspiratorial thinking.

In Chapter 4, I attempt to frame contemporary right-wing nationalist populism. I explore its roots and map both the birth and development of populist movements in post-war era Europe. I start with discussing a few underlying concepts, such as populism, nationalism and fascism. Next, I discuss the international architecture built after Second World War and its institutional setup, which many nationalist populists have built some of their most persistent CTs around. Then, I discuss the evolvement of cultural racism and separate between three main waves of far-right populism in the post-war era. Lastly, I identify the winning formula of the present conspiratorial far-right in the West.

In Chapter 5, I examine common tropes of CTs and populism and attempt to frame populist CTs and identify how they are applied in politics. I move on to separate those individuals in society that merely subscribe to CTs from the political actors that produce and promote them for political gain, who here are in focus. The chapter concludes with studying four powerful conspiratorial and populist actors in contemporary politics. First, I discuss those upheld by the *Front National* in France. Second, I address anti-Western theories in post-Soviet Russia. Third, I look into CTs spread by Donald Trump in the USA. Last, I turn to exploring further anti-EU CTs upheld, for example, by prominent players in the UK Brexit debate.

In Chapter 6, I explore the CT of an Islamist takeover of Europe, a theory which can be referred to as the *Eurabia* doctrine—the Islamization of Europe. I start with a short look into migration of recent years and the general nature of anti-Muslim CTs before discussing a selection of three specific cases. First, I pick up the discussion from the previous chapter around Brexit in the UK, focusing on the anti-Muslim and anti-immigrant rhetoric in the campaign. Next, I discuss anti-Muslim politics of Donald Trump in America, mentioned briefly above, and also the neo-Nazi protests in Charlottesville in 2017. Lastly, in a more lengthier analysis, I examine anti-Muslim discourse across the Nordic countries.

In Chapter 7, I turn to discussing how populist political CTs are transmitted. The recent decline in trust of mainstream media and increased importance of online media has proved to be a fertile ground for the spread of CTs. Here, a specific focus will, thus, be on the distribution of populist CTs through fake news on the Internet, primarily on social media. I touch on conspiratorial fake news stories in the Brexit debate and then discuss further those upheld in the US and in Russia.

In Chapter 8, I will bring the discussion in the previous chapters to conclusion and analyse how populists use CTs to advance their politics.

References

Barkun, M. (2013). *A culture of conspiracy: Apocalyptic visions in contemporary America*. Berkeley: University of California Press.
Bergmann, E. (2017). *Nordic nationalism and right-wing populist politics: Imperial relationships and national sentiments*. London: Palgrave Macmillan.
Breivik, A. (2011). *2083—A European declaration of independence*. London.
Brotherton, R. (2015). *Suspisious minds—Why we belief conspiracy theories*. New York: Bloomsbury.
Butter, M., & Knight, P. (2016). Bridging the great divide: Conspiracy theory research for the 21st century. *Sage—Diogenes*. https://doi.org/10.1177/0392192116669289.
Byford, J. (2011). *Conspiracy theories: A critical introduction*. Basingstoke: Palgrave Macmillan.
deHaven-Smith, L. (2014). *Conspiracy theory in America*. Texas: University of Texas Press.
DeLillo, D. (1978). *Running dog*. New York: Knopf.
Eco, U. (1995, June 22). Ur-Fascism. *The New York Review of Books*. Retrieved from nybooks.com.
Evans-Pritchard, E. E. (1937). Witchcraft, oracles and magic among the Azande. In M. Robben (Ed.), *Death, mourning, and burial*. Hoboken: Wiley.
Hofstadter, R. (1964). *The paranoid style in American politics*. New York: Vintage Books.
MacAskill, E., Borger, J., Hopkins, N., Davies, N., & Ball, J. (2013, June 21). GCHQ taps fibre-optic cables for secret access to world's communications. *The Guardian*. London.

Oliver, J. E., & Rahn, W. M. (2016). Rise of the Trumpenvolk: Populism in the 2016 election. *The ANNALS of the American Academy of Political and Social Science, 667*(1), 189–206.

Oliver, J. E., & Wood, T. J. (2014). Conspiracy theories and the paranoid style(s) of mass opinion. *American Journal of Political Science, 58*(4), 952–966.

Pipes, D. (1999). *Conspiracy: How the paranoid style flourishes and where it comes from.* New York: Simon & Schuster.

Popper, K. S. (2012). *The open society and its enemies.* Abingdon-on-Thames: Routledge.

Seierstad, A. (2015). *One of us: The story of Anders Breivik and the massacre in Norway.* New York: Farrar, Straus and Giroux.

Snyder, T. (2017). *On tyranny: Twenty lessons from the twentieth century.* New York: Tim Duggan Books.

van Prooijen, J.-W., Krouwel, A. P. M., & Pollet, T. V. (2015). Political extremism predicts belief in conspiracy theories. *Social Psychological and Personality Science, 6*(5), 570–578.

Wodak, R. (1995). Critical linguistics and critical discourse analysis. In J. Verscheuren, J. O. Östman, & E. Versluys (Eds.), *Handbook of pragmatics 1995* (pp. 204–210). Amsterdam: John Benjamins.

2

Kinds of Conspiracy Theories

In series of public talks and via distribution of audio recordings, a young evangelist, John Wayne Todd, attempted in the 1970s to unravel a diabolical plot he claimed was already underway by several malevolent forces, who were in the process of taking over control in the world, mainly centred around the notorious Illuminati. Time was running out, he claimed, as the plan would be completed by autumn 1979. Todd insisted that he had inside knowledge of the conspiracy, as he himself had previously belonged to the so-called Druid Council of Thirteen, which behind the scenes, had the task of executing the decisions of what he called the Rothschild tribunal. Todd claimed to have been raised as a witch, before being borne again as Christian. The Council, he said, consisted of a band of rich families in finance and global trade, secretly ruling in seclusion, far away from the visible society (see Barkun 2013).

In addition to the Rothschild family, Todd maintained that many other influential forces united in the self-serving evil network. This modern version of the Illuminati included, for example, both the Rockefeller and the Kennedy families. The network also reached far into government agencies, such as the central banks of England, France and the United States. Todd's version of the Illuminati controlled churches, political parties, governments and major international institutions.

© The Author(s) 2018
E. Bergmann, *Conspiracy & Populism*, https://doi.org/10.1007/978-3-319-90359-0_2

In his talks and recordings, Todd described what he said was a *Plan for World Takeover* (see Arendt 2014). He maintained that the Illuminati had twice before in recent history tried to take over full control of the world, first in Napoleon's time and again during the First World War. And now, another attempt was underway, he said. The young born again evangelist explained that only around five thousand people worldwide knew of the true purpose of the Illuminati and its world domination conspiracy. Amongst many components of his detailed theory was, for example, his revelation that businessman Philippe Rothschild had ordered neo-liberal writer Ayn Rand, who Todd claimed was his mistress, to write the plot in code and print it in her novel, *Atlas Shrugged*, published in 1957. The characters in the book, Todd claimed, were code names for real individuals or companies. Todd asserted that it was only by accident that Rand's novel became as well-known as it proved to be after publication—for some reason, only that aspect had, as it seems, not been part of the grand master plan.

Todd maintained that the Illuminati intended to rule over six societal areas: religion, politics, economics, education, military and society. He described how Philippe Rothschild had on 1 August 1972 sent over to the Council of Thirteen reports and papers, which in addition to the usual pay-off notes and progress reports, included a world domination takeover plan. The first action on Rothschild's list, Todd said, was to remove both the US president and vice president. Secondly, the Republican successor would willingly surrender power to the Democratic Party. After being inaugurated, the Democrat President would revoke the federal gun law, remove tax exemptions for churches and ban people from converting from one religion or faith to another. Next, the President would instate a martial law act, which would allow him in times of national emergency to suspend the Constitution, Congress, and indeed all instruments of national economic oversight. The president would then go on to make every citizen completely dependent on the government, for instance, by falsely creating a fuel and food shortage, and by confiscating all guns.

Collectively, Todd claimed, this would lead to a Charles Manson-type Helter Skelter state of affairs—an apocalyptic war arising from increased social tensions. Rouge gangs would be unleashed on the public, creating chaos by bombing church buildings, and raping and murdering innocent people in the streets. When time was ripe, Israel would then, according to the plot, start World War III. While the world was crashing, key figures of the Illuminati would, however, safely wait their time in the Bermuda Triangle—which, by the way, Todd claimed was coded in Ayn Rand's book as being the US state of Colorado.

In this terrifyingly violent and chaotic world collapse, instigated by the Illuminati, the devastated public would, in desperation, be calling on authorities to reinstate order, at any cost. As a response, all non-military vehicles, trucks, trains, planes, and ships, would stop moving. Finally, the government would declare martial law and send in the National Guard to instate order. In conclusion, this New World Order dictatorship, Todd insisted was already firmly on the cards, would be ruled from Jerusalem.

John Todd's vast and fanciful CT was amazingly detailed and obviously the essence of it could with all conventional reason easily be debunked. Still, many right-wing groups around the US, and, indeed, around the world, adopted his worldview (Barkun 2013). In 1981, a summary of Todd's incredible descriptions was published in a pamphlet titled *Witchcraft and the Illuminati* in 1999. The publisher of the pamphlet was a heavily armed militant far-right Christian identity commune named The Covenant, the Sword, and the Arm of the Lord. In 1984, Todd was placed on five years' probation for incest and in 1988, he was convicted for rape and sentenced to 30 years in prison.

Todd's theory of the vast Illuminati conspiracy might have been more far-fetched and perhaps more imaginative than many other accounts of this notorious secret society, but tales of these kinds and many other forms of a New World Order have survived through centuries. And although most people probably dismiss them as mere fabrications of unstable persons on the fringes of society, they have still often had significant influence on political beliefs around the globe.

As will be discussed in the following chapter, examining the internal design and nature of CTs, they are of various kinds and sorts and can be categorized in many different ways. Here, I provide a short general overview of some of the most common CTs upheld in the public domain.

New World Order

Conspiracy theories of a New World Order, of a kind like the one John Todd created and upheld, are a category of their own—with several versions floating around insisting that the world is run—or is about to be—by a concealed external elite trying to create some form of world domination. Usually, these are holistic and overreaching explanations, fitting a series of events—some including the entirety of public life—into a single plot. Most often, there is said to be a globalist agenda of establishing an authoritarian world government, which is to replace the system of sovereign nation-states.

These sorts of theories can be found in both religious and secular versions. For instance, in his celebrated book, *Brave New World*, Aldous Huxley (1932) paints a rosy picture of a utopian world of peace and prosperity, no wars and no poverty. Underneath, however, looms the threat of the coming tyrannical dictatorship.

New World Order theories also come in the form of global elites manipulating not only national governments worldwide but also controlling international organizations such as the European Union (EU), International Monetary Fund, United Nations and the World Bank (WB).

These types of theories have already been floating around for more than two centuries. In contemporary times, they were, however, fuelled and driven much further when US President George H. Bush voiced his vision of a New World Order taking hold in wake of the Cold War. His address was delivered to a joint session of Congress on 11 September 1990. Bush meant to describe a more peaceful and prosperous post-Cold-War era, based on rule of law, and a new political environment of diverse coexisting nations. In his speech to Congress, he called for a 'new era freer from the threat of terror, stronger in the pursuit of justice and more secure in the quest for peace. An era in which the nations of the world, east and west, north and south, can prosper and live in harmony.'

Still, many conspiracy theorists took the president's address as proof of malignant intentions on his part and his hidden collaborators. The conspiracy theorists believed that they were behind the scenes working on establishing a united world government dominating the entire earth. Termination of all dissidents would follow, they said. Many of these New World Order theories swirling around in the wake of his speech, made reference to his past as member of the Yale student society, Skulls and Bones, and his function as head of the CIA before becoming President. These connections were highlighted in order to underpin an argument of his ties to a covert cabal of dark forces.

The dramatic changes around the collapse of communism and the dissolution of the Soviet Union, indeed, opened up a new space in the conspiratorial milieu in the West. The Soviets had for a long time been presented as the main enemy of the West, and many anti-communist CTs of evil deeds by the Eastern bloc thrived during the Cold War. And, now, suddenly, the enemy was gone—had vanished into thin air. As Barkun argues (2013), this led to a vacuum, which was increasingly being filled by New World Order theories of the far-right.

One section of this sphere revolved around stories of alien control of the government, the so-called UFO logists. Amongst these was, for example, a theory upheld by Milton William Cooper (1991) in his exposé publication, *Behold a Pale Horse*. In his book, Cooper entangles extra-terrestrials with the Bilderberg group, the Illuminati and Protocols of the Elders of Zion—all are discussed further later in this chapter—into a world dominating dictatorial order. He maintained that their Luciferian themes had even been slipped into the Great Seal of the United States, '*Novous ordo seclorum*,' which he claimed really meant 'New World Order' (see Barkun 2013).

Amongst common themes of New World Order theories, were for example, tales of black helicopters patrolling the globe, that authorities were running a network of hidden concentration camps around the world, where they incarcerated dissidents, and that they were keeping tabs on the public through secret mind control programs.

Antichrist

Michael Barkun (2013) distinguishes between two types of New World Order CTs. One revolves around millenarian Christianity, i.e. speculations of an apocalyptic end of time and the rise of diabolic figures such as the Antichrist. The other kind centres on secret societies ruling the world, rather than governments, which I discuss further in the next segment.

Theories of existence of an Antichrist usually revolve around tales of some Satanic figure seizing control of the world, of a diabolical actor becoming leader of a world dictatorship. Through history, many political leaders have been pointed to as potentially being the Antichrists, including the obvious choices, such as interwar fascist leaders in Europe: Adolf Hitler and Benito Mussolini. More recently, leaders like US President Barack Obama and Pope John Paul II have been accused of being the Antichrist.

Another version of this type centres on institutions or associations being the Antichrist. In the 1920s, several conspiracy theorists insisted that the League of Nations was only a façade, that behind it was a hidden purpose. They insisted that the League was indeed a vehicle for preparing the coming of the Antichrist and seizing control on Earth (Fuller 1996). Some of the post-World War II international constructions have been suspected of being the Antichrist, for example, the United Nations and the EU and its predecessors. Many saw the EU as resurrection of the Roman Empire, this time as a European super-state led by the Antichrist. For some reason, theories of an Antichrist indeed often centre on resurrection of the Roman Empire.

In the 1980s, these beliefs were, for example, being entangled into suspicions of the computer as an instrument of the Antichrist; some viewed this new and revolutionary invention as being the Antichrist. In one version, the Antichrist was said to be a computer kept deep within the European institutional apparatus in Brussels, keeping track of everyone in the world (Boyer 1994).

Leading up to the 2008 US presidential election, several anti-Barack Obama CTs were afloat in the public domain, as will be discussed later in this chapter, including the before mentioned preposterous claim that he was, indeed, the Antichrist (Posner 2008). Amongst those believing the story was a young Mexican-American named Oscar Ortega, who in November 2011 shot at the White House in an utterly hopeless attempt of assassinating the Antichrist President, illegally occupying the Oval office. Later, it was revealed that Ortega was mentally ill, and that he had been under the influence of the anti-governmental message upheld by the notorious Texas-based conservative talk show host and professional conspiracy theorist, Alex Jones. Ortega had, for example, watched Jones film titled *The Obama Deception* (Yardley 2011).

Early Illuminati

Perhaps the most tenacious secular New World Order CT centres on the mysterious Illuminati. Tales of this secret society are found in many forms and have repeatedly cropped up in different periods and in various versions. Established out of the Freemasons and Jesuit groups, this brotherhood—which only later on gained its notoriety—was founded in Bavaria in 1776, now located within Germany, by a canon law professor, Adam Weishaupt. Initially, it was named the Order of the Illuminati, later referred to as the Illuminati. The name refers to the Enlightenment and the stated purpose was opposing 'superstition, obscurantism, religious influence over public life, and abuses of state power' (see Dulmen 1992). Its main goal was, in other words, the establishment of a secular legal order, which was to replace previous royal and religious based polities.

The Illuminati was based on an elaborate hierarchy. The operations and ceremonies were heavily decorated with rituals and securely based on secrecy. The purpose of the society was to protect the society from infiltration of hostile government agents and also to mould the members into becoming a powerful elite, who could push the grandiose agenda of the brotherhood into action. The actual secret society survived only for roughly a decade before being dissolved in or around 1787. At its peak, it is estimated that around 2500 people, mainly German speakers, belonged to it (Barkun 2013).

The Illuminati was founded on ideals from the Enlightenment, mainly on secularising governance. Thus, it was perhaps not, in itself, too far-fetched to imagine that the principals of the French revolution might have been influenced by their aims, or at least inspired by similar ones. The Illuminati had, though, been dissolved well before the tumult started. Still, rumours of the secret society having prompted the revolution were soon spreading and some insisted that the order of the Illuminati had never died. A few further insisted that the allegedly dissolved secret society was also responsible for the American Revolution that followed. Some went on to advance the theory far beyond all previous tales and maintained that the Illuminati was not only still alive, but had been elevated to ruling the entire world.

Two early publications were influential in spreading the story of the Illuminati orchestrating the French revolution. One was *Proof of a Conspiracy* by John Robison (1798). Another was written by Augustin de Barruel (2010) titled *Memoirs, Illustrating the History of Jacobinism*, first published in 1797. Barruel insisted that the French revolution had indeed been orchestrated by these dark forces who opposed both the Church and Crown and promoted instead freedom and equality.

Barkun (2013) shows that the spread of these and similar tales of the Illuminati deliberately orchestrating the French and American revolutions first reached wider audience around 1830, when both of these books were reprinted by actors who insisted that they provided proof of a master conspiracy to 'enslave all people in Europe and America.'

Interwar Illuminati

A second iteration of Illuminati CTs was instigated in the interwar years, mainly via publications of two English writers, Nesta H. Webster (1921) and Lady Queensborough, also known as Edith Starr Miller (2009). In addition to adopting from Robison and Barruel the insistence mentioned before, that the Illuminati was responsible for the French revolution, both writers also maintained that world history could, indeed, only be made sense of by taking into account how it was controlled by a string of secret societies. In this fresh version of a New World Order, the Illuminati was said to be only one of many components. In this version of the story, their collaborators included, for example, the Knights Templar, Cabbalists, Rosicrucians, and the Carbonari, which all were colluding in constructing the global dictatorship. Most importantly, for future development of the theory, both women insisted that Jews were controlling the entire vast network. Lady Queensborough furthermore warned that Jews were already behind the scenes systematically gathering under their control most of the world's financial resources. It was mainly in this version that the CT of the Illuminati travelled across the Atlantic and became widespread also in America.

All sorts of events were now being entangled into this malignant web of world domination, including, for example, the Russian revolution, and, thus, subsequently the communist Soviet Union. Hence, as Barkun (2013) has pointed out, proponents of the theory now maintained that 'to fight Jews was simultaneously to fight both communism and the Illuminati,' who discursively were both, as a result, seen as being merged into a single entity.

Contemporary Illuminati

A third iteration of tales of an Illuminati conspiracy was running off the printers soon after the Second World War. In view of the Birch Society,[1] the Illuminati were now being entangled into a breath of evil deeds. Some insisted that they had created nationalism, fascism, Nazism and communism, and that they were, thus, responsible for both of the devastating world wars (Barkun 2013). Alongside increased suspicion of communists working behind the scenes in America, tales of the Illuminati entered the mainstream in the 1960s and 1970s. From there, these stories spread further around the entire Western world.

In his book, *None Dare Call It Conspiracy*, published by the Birch Society, Larry Abraham (1973) set out to unravel a plot of evil doers who were well underway with their planning of establishing a United Socialist States of America. Abraham maintained that other countries of the world would then also be forced into the new global dictatorial state. Like John Todd did later, as was discussed at the beginning of this chapter, Abraham also put the international banking family, the Rothschilds, firmly at the centre of the conspiracy he aimed to expose.

Many other actors have as well been associated with similar grand plots of world domination. On that same basis, evangelist conspiracy theorist Texe Marrs, for example, insisted that the Illuminati was merely an umbrella 'of one gigantic, unified global network known collectively as the Secret Brotherhood' (cited in Barkun 2013).

One of the most widely distributed contemporary accounts of the Illuminati was published by Pat Robertson (1991), simply titled *The New World Order*. Typical for that sort of a CT, the villains exposed in the book were said to be well on their way to undermining both Christianity and American liberties, before establishing their evil world government. This trope has indeed become one of the most common themes of CT's revolving around the notorious Illuminati.

Protocols of the Elders of Zion

Several CTs revolve around religion, often aiming to unravel outright religious plots. Indeed, religion also lies beneath many tales of the Illuminati. Most commonly, the secret brotherhood is suspected of setting out to destroy both the Crown and Christianity.

This was the version often upheld by the American far-right, where tales of the Illuminati were merged with anti-Semitic CTs. Often the two were being entangled into stories of The Protocols of the Learned Elders of Zion. John Todd, discussed at the beginning of the chapter, was, for example, weaving out of exactly this same thread when insisting that the Illuminati world government, which he maintained was on the cards, would be ruled from Jerusalem.

As was established in previous discussion, anti-Semitism has for centuries been at the centre of many of the most persistent CTs afloat both in Europe and in the USA. Jews have been suspected of various covert evil deeds, for example, of poisoning Christian drinking wells and killing Jesus Christ, to name just two of the classics. Others have revolved around their alleged control over international finance, for instance, those insisting that the Jewish Rothschild family controlled both Wall Street and the US Federal Reserve System (Levy et al. 2005). Perhaps one of the most interesting anti-Semitist tale in modern times was told on the RationalWiki website, of a Yiddish secret society called Goy Cabal using Wikipedia as a misinformation tool in advancing their plot of dominating the world.

Holocaust denial is another example of anti-Semitic CTs. This is the insistence that reports of Nazis running termination camps systematically killing Jews were merely a hoax; that these stories were deliberately fabricated and spread in order to rally support for the creation of the state of Israel (Shermer et al. 2009).

Anti-Semitic ideas date back centuries. One interesting example is found in the Norwegian constitution that was being drafted in the wake of the Napoleonic wars in 1814. The document included stipulations banning Jews, Jesuits and monkish orders (Dyrendal 2017).

In the nineteenth century, a more sophisticated and comprehensive anti-Semitic theory was evolving, insisting that Jews, in collaboration with Freemasons, were collectively plotting world domination. The proof of this Jewish New World Order conspiracy was said to be found in a secret text titled The Protocols of the Elders of Zion. The Protocols are transcripts of speeches presented to an assembly of senior Jewish leaders at the end of the nineteenth century. Later, another version of the same insistence was spread around in tales of what was referred to as Zionist Occupation Government (ZOG).

Allegedly, the Protocols fletch out a plan of subverting governments and institutions under Jewish control and constructing a Zionist-led world government. On the grounds of the Protocols, Jews were suspected of standing behind revolutions and rebellions around Europe. In Russia, Jews in the nineteenth century were suspected of subverting political stability, for example, through financial actions. This theory became more widespread throughout the Arab world (De Poli 2014).

In the late nineteenth and early twentieth century, there was a widespread suspicion in many European countries that these nations were threatened by a shadow elite of Jews, Masons and communists seeking world domination. Anti-semitism was though not confined to Europe. In 1920, Victor Marsden's (2011) English translations of the Protocols were being distributed widely in the USA, with the insistence that they provided proof of a Jewish conspiracy, working at assuming all power on Earth. In this version, Jews were said to be seizing control with help of a college of co-conspirators. Their collaborators included Masonic actors, and thus, also involved the Illuminati. Here, several versions of New World Order CTs are merged into a unified tale revolving around the Protocols. In his notorious manifesto, *Mein Kampf*, Adolf Hitler (1925) for example centres his suspicions of Jews on the Protocols.

After World War II, CTs around the Protocols became increasingly discredited and were widely dismissed as being anti-Semitic. With the atrocities of a Jewish genocide by the Nazi regime coming to light, most decent people did not want to be associated with anti-semitism.

However, even though tales around the Protocols and ZOG had receded in the wake of the war, they were never extinct. In his book, *Fourth Reich of the Rich*, Des Griffin (1976), for example, describes the Protocols as the 'Long Range Master Plan' of the Illuminati, in which a 'small group of immensely wealthy, diabolically crafty and extremely influential men plan to subvert and pervert the leadership in all strata of society in order to attain their goals.'

Anti-Catholic

In many Protestant dominated countries, suspicions of Catholics and the Vatican have been alive for centuries. Several of these tales were in line with some of the New World Order theories discussed earlier, and thus, also include familiar elements such as the Knights Templar, Jesuits and indeed the Illuminati as well as other secret societies.

Allegations against some Catholic societies, for example, included accusations of them being engaged in Satanism, human sacrifice, orgies and black masses. Others insisted that the Vatican was responsible for communism, Nazism, and the First and Second World Wars, in addition to the assassinations of both Abraham Lincoln and John F. Kennedy (Wylie 2002).

In England, allegations of the so-called Popish Plot were spreading in the seventeenth century. These were fictitious accusations of Jesuits planning to assassinate King Charles II in order to pave the way for his Catholic brother to ascend to the throne, King James II. The fabricated story led to hysteria in Britain, and several killings and expulsions of many Catholics from the country (Popish Plot 2017).

City fires also seem to spur CTs around them. I have already mentioned how Emperor Nero was suspected of having set blaze to Rome in CE 64. Another theory of a similar kind blamed Catholics for the Great fire of London in 1666.

In the seventeenth and the eighteenth centuries, Catholics were, in many Protestant dominated countries in Europe, increasingly seen as a fifth column, that is, as infiltrators covertly aiming to incorporating these countries under the control of the Vatican. More recently, the protestant leader in Northern Ireland, Ian Paisley, once denounced Pope John Paul II as being the Antichrist (Kyle 2009).

Similarly, in America, several CTs have been afloat fearing a Catholic takeover, insisting that Catholic migrants were aiming to bring the US government under the auspices of the Vatican. In 1835, Samuel Morse (2007) published a book titled *Foreign Conspiracies Against the Liberties of the United States*. He saw Catholics as part of a network of wider conspiratorial groups operating out of Vienna, who were working to move the USA under the authority of the Habsburg Empire. Even during the 1960 US presidential election campaign, reverend Billy Graham voiced his concerns that John F. Kennedy would be a Vatican infiltrator in the White House (Balmer 2011).

Amongst the most far reaching anti-Catholic CTs, was upheld by cartoonist Jack Chick. He, for example, maintained that the Vatican kept a secret file on every Protestant church member around the world, for use in future persecutions. Chick insisted that in addition to operating the Illuminati, the Vatican was also running international finance, the Mafia and the New Age movement, as well as many communist movements, the Ku Klux Klan, Jehovah's Witnesses and Mormonism (Akin 2004).

As if this was not enough, Chick also insisted that Catholics had, in effect, also created Islam. In his version of a Vatican Islam Conspiracy, the aim was both, he said, to destroy other Christian churches and Jews.

Holy Grail

A fascinating conspiracy theory revolves around the Bible and the mysterious Holy Grail, the insistence that much of the holy book is merely a deception to conceal an ancient secret. This theory was, for example, dramatized in Dan Brown's (2009) novel, *The Da Vinci Code*. The theory maintains that initial tales of Jesus Christ describe him as being simply a mortal and earthly leader of a similar kind to all other human beings. Advocates of this theory maintain that those stories were suppressed after his death and that the ones finally included in the Bible were carefully selected to falsely highlight his divine nature as Messiah. This version not only insists that Jesus was married to a woman, Mary Magdalena, but also that he had fathered a child. Perhaps the most interesting aspect of the story is the claim that descendants of Christ still populate the Earth.

As the story goes, the Church deliberately and systematically deceived its worshippers in order to secure its authority as the link between humans and the divine world. It does this by upholding a fabricated tale of the divinity of Jesus Christ. In Dan Brown's novel, the truth is still kept within a secret society called the Priory of Sion, which at the right time is meant to unravel the deception. The revelation would be to the detriment of the Church, which would lose its authority if the truth ever came to light. It is thus in the firm interest of the Church to suppress the truth by any means necessary. According to this theory, the Holy Grail is not the goblet Christ drank from during the last supper. Rather, the Holy Grail is understood to be the supressed truth of Christ having merely been a human and mortal husband to a woman and a father of a child. The CT here, is, thus, of covert forces within the Church suppressing the truth.

Anti-Islam

As will be discussed further in Chapter 6, several CTs revolve around Islam and Muslims infiltrating the West. A common trope among those is that religious minorities like Muslims in Europe and in America are working to oppress Christians. Another is of the aforementioned notorious Norwegian right-wing terrorist, Anders Behring Breivik, secretly being a pawn of the Islamists.

Thirdly, the so-called *Birther* movement in America claims that former President Barack Obama was born in Kenya and therefore never eligible to be US President. Many within the movement furthermore claimed that he, in fact, was in secret a Muslim.

Yet another anti-Islam CT, maintains that a Muslim caliphate created the horrendous 2014 Ebola epidemic in West Africa, and planned to use the virus as weapon, for example, by blowing up an Ebola victim on the busy Times Square in New York City. Perhaps the most far-fetched on the list, was a claim that Islamic fascists inhabit the centre of the moon.

Contrary to these, there also exist CTs indicating that Western forces were systematically demonising Muslims to advance support for right-wing nationalists. Among them were tales of the assassination of eight journalists at the *Charlie Hebdo* comic magazine in Paris in January 2015, being staged by the French government as a pretext for a crack-down on the Muslim population.

Bilderberg Group

Concealed cabals aiming to establish a New World Order are not the only groups that have been suspected of sinister plots. The real-life Bilderberg group has, for instance, long been a favourite culprit of conspiracy theorists. It is named after a meeting of the world elite gathering at the Bilderberg hotel in the Netherlands, where a select group of European and American businessmen, politicians and academics first met in 1952. The group has since run a series of meetings around the world.

The Bilderberg's initial purpose was in strengthening relations between the USA and Europe and preventing another world war. They held a neo-liberal agenda, and one of their goals was to 'bolster a consensus around free market Western capitalism and its interests around the globe' (BBC News 2011).

Throughout its existence, contradictory theories have been floating around about their sinister aims. From the political left, the Bilderberg group has been accused of plotting to impose a global capitalist domination, while on the political right they have been suspected of conspiring to instate a one world communist style government and planned economy (Sanburn 2016).

Phyllis Schlafly (1964) for example, wrote in her book *A Choice, Not an Echo*, that the Republican Party in America was secretly controlled by the Bilderberg group, whose globalist agenda was imposing world communism. In 2010, Cuban revolutionist leader, Fidel Castro, on the other hand wrote in the Cuban communist newspaper, *Granma*, that the Bilderberg group was secretly aiming at installing 'a world government that knows no borders and is not accountable to anyone but its own self.' (cited in Dice 2015).

Deep State

Another version suspecting a malignant covert elite ruling a nation or region, is the theory of a deep state. The term coins the belief that society is not ruled by its official authorities, but, instead, by a secret band of hidden potentates, such as a bureaucratic class controlling everything behind the scenes. These sorts of theories were simmering mainly in Middle Eastern and North African politics since the 1960s and can, surely, hold some truth to them. In Turkey, the term *derin devlet* refers to a cartel of politicians and bureaucrats in different governmental branches together with high-ranking military officials, as well as organised crime, covertly controlling the country (*The Economist* 2017).

With rise of the Tea Party in the USA and the election of Donald Trump as president in 2016, this theory was imported into America where it found renewed prominence. In the American version, the idea of a deep state refers to a covert secret elite who is systematically, and in a coordinated manner, manipulating the country's politics and government. In the USA, political pundits have tended to use this notion interchangeably with the bureaucracies of the military and spy agencies (ibid.).

Proponents of these theories include, for instance, author Peter Dale Scott, *Breitbart News*, and US President Donald Trump, who for example, described the deep state as 'real, illegal and a threat to national security' (cited in Porter 2017). In a 2017 poll, *ABC News* and *The Washington Post* found that almost half of Americans believed in a conspiratorial *deep state* in the US (ibid.).

Assassinations—Dead *and* Alive

One common cluster of CTs revolves around claims of governments or other powerful forces secretly murdering people. One insists that Princess Diana was assassinated by a British governmental agent to prevent her from marrying Muslim Dodi Al-Fayed (Burns 2008). Others maintain that the US government killed John F. Kennedy, Malcom X and Martin Luther King. Yet another claim is that Vice President Andrew Johnson was behind the Abraham Lincoln assassination. There are also theories floating around involving Lincoln being killed in a Jesuit conspiracy.

A more imaginative theory accuses Bill and Hillary Clinton of killing 50 people, private citizens. Here, we can also mention those CTs asserting that the CIA shot down the Trans World Airlines Flight 800 that exploded and crashed into the Atlantic Ocean near New York in 1996.

The flip side to these kinds of CTs, are tales of people reportedly dead being still alive. Amongst those are, for example, claims that Osama Bin Laden was not killed by the US army, and, thus, completely countering the aforementioned theory of him being long dead, prior to the reported assassination.

JFK CTs are probably amongst the most widespread. Opinion polls have indicated that an ample majority of Americans don't believe the official account of events, i.e. that John F. Kennedy was killed by Lee Harvey Oswald acting alone. These stories were amplified with the release of Oliver Stone's conspiratorial film, *JFK*, in 1991.

Deceptions, Disasters, Diseases and Medicine

Many theories include tales of political leaders covertly operating to advance their positions. One involves the Ronald Reagan presidential campaign making a deal with the Iranian government to not release the US hostages, who they would keep until after Reagan was elected President in 1980, as that would damage his Democrat opponent.

Amongst the most common types of CTs are tales of malignant deceptions of governments and other powerful forces. Several of those revolve around diseases and medicine. One of the most popular CTs claims that a cure for cancer actually exists but is being suppressed by the government; another involves a cover-up in the UK, in which authorities were obscuring knowledge of childhood cancer levels being ten times the country's average along the North Wales coast.

A similar theory maintains that scientists and politicians were covering up the knowledge that mercury in vaccines causes autism, something that has long been scientifically debunked.

A cluster of such CTs revolve around wicked science. Many have, for example, been afloat around HIV and AIDS. One indicates that the virus was created by the CIA and deliberately spread by the World Health Organisation (WHO) via polio inoculations in Africa. Supposedly this was done in order to reduce the world population. Another version insists that scientists and politicians were covering up evidence of AIDS not being caused by HIV infection (Kalichman 2009).

Yet another version insists that the CIA had created HIV and AIDS by scientists in laboratories and that the virus was specifically aimed at the black community along with other undesirable groups, such as homosexuals. In a survey published in 2005, around half of African Americans respondents indeed accepted the claim that authorities were taking measures to prevent the black community from growing larger (Bird and Bogart 2005).

Of a similar kind is the insistence that the swine flu outbreak in 2009 was engineered by the American government, with the aim of declaring martial law, herding everyone into FEMA concentration camps, and forcibly vaccinating people with the virus in order to deliberately depopulate the Earth so that the masterminds of the New World Order could take control (Potok and Terry 2015). In a speech to the General Assembly of the United Nations in 2009, Muammar Gaddafi of Libya, for instance, said that the swine flu virus was manufactured in laboratories (cited in Byford 2011).

FEMA, the US government run Federal Emergency Management Agency, has indeed been the subject of many conspiracy theories, for example, of running concentration camps, similar to those in

Nazi Germany. In the film, *The X-files* (1998), based on the widely watched television series of the same name, FEMA became a target of a widespread CT. The film's main conspiracy theorist protagonist, Dr. Kurzweil, predicts that after the government issued state of emergency, all federal agencies would fall under control of FEMA. As Barkun (2013) points out, this belief, which previously had only existed in fringe extreme-right groups, was now exposed to millions of mainstream movie viewers.

False Flag Operations—And 9/11

Theories of false flag operations are another separate category. Most commonly, these are tales of horrendous acts covertly carried out by authorities and being blamed on others. Some of these tales have later been deemed credible. German historians are, for example, still debating the plausibility of the 1933 German parliament, *Reichstag* arson being a false flag operation of the Nazis, pinning the blame on communists.

Perhaps the most persistent and influential false flag CT in contemporary times has arisen around the terrorist attacks in the USA on 9 November 2001, killing 2996 people. The 9/11 event was of a monumental proportion and importance, not only for the USA, but also for the entire Western world. Within weeks, all sorts of CTs were cropping up, countering the conventional account that the towers were brought down by 19 Al Qaida terrorists from mostly Saudi Arabia and also the United Arab Emirates, Egypt and Lebanon.

These theories came in many versions. Most commonly, they insisted that US President George W. Bush and British Prime Minister Tony Blair knew about the attacks in advance and let them happen. This resembles the CT believed by many Americans, that in the Second World War President Roosevelt knew about the Pearl Harbour attack in advance, and let it happen.

One version even insists that the US government, in fact, staged the 9/11 attacks; that the towers were brought down by controlled demolition. Yet another version indicates that UFOs had appeared near the buildings and that it was, thus, in fact, an extra-terrestrial attack.

Many much more specific theories were also floating around. One explains in detail how the World Trade Centre Building 7 was purposely detonated. Another insists that the Pentagon was not hit by an aircraft, but by a US missile. In addition to claiming that the US government staged the attacks in an inside job—perhaps similar to what Emperor Nero was accused of regarding the Great Fire of Rome—many other actors have been implicated in the attack, they include, for example, the Israeli government, the Illuminati and the Rothschild family.

Many of the usual suspects were rolling out their favourite explanations. New World Order conspiracy theorists took it as proof of malignant forces seizing domination through terrorism. Texe Marrs did not wait long before blaming it on the Illuminati and Patrick H. Bellringer said that an organization called Khazarian Zionist Bolshevik (KZB) was responsible for the attack (for more, see Barkun 2013). The far-right publication, *Free American*, alluded to it being a false flag operation, a pretence to implement a military police state—of course run by FEMA. And perhaps, unsurprisingly, many millennialists saw the 9/11 event as an indication of the end of time, that Armageddon was nearing.

In fact, almost the entire gallery of conspiracy theorists around the world were competing in implicating their favourite culprits as being responsible for the attacks—no matter where the evidence pointed to. Unsurprisingly, Milton William Cooper (2001), for example, pinned the blame on the Bush family, insisting that they were the main beneficiaries of the attacks alongside the oil industry, the military-industrial complex, the UN and Israel. He went on to say that 'tyranny in the name of security will benefit and rule over the American People.'

Many scholars have mapped how the 9/11 event served to transfer CTs further into the mainstream than perhaps ever before (see for example Barkun 2013). In fact, there is now a vast and far-reaching literature widely available in mainstream circulation solely devoted to questioning official accounts and offering alternative versions of what happened that Tuesday morning.

In 2006, a selection of scholars and pseudo-academics came together in a group called Scholars for 9/11 Truth and Justice. Amongst other activities, they founded the *Journal of 9/11 Studies*. Many of the papers published in the journal raised issues with official accounts of the event, questioning explanations of how the buildings came down and some offered alternative accounts of what had happened.

Many, for example David Ray Griffin (2006), indeed insisted that the event was a false flag operation, concocted by the Bush administration to provide justification for invading Afghanistan and Iraq. Others, for example, Peter Dale Scott (2013), drew similarities between 9/11 and the John F. Kennedy assassination, classifying both as what he called 'deep events.' Those, he said, were events that the mainstream media avoided and were only studied by scholars of what he referred to as 'deep history.' Scott identified similar patterns around both events, including senior government officials being away and fast identification of perpetrators. He insisted that both events had a common cause, serving the interests of 'forces lobbying permanently for increased militarization.' Another account upheld by Kevin Ryan (2017) insisted that powerful office tenants in the World Trade Centre had been in on the plot.

Many other CTs revolve around 9/11, for example, the one mentioned in the introduction to this book, upheld by US President Donald Trump, insisting that Muslims in New Jersey were celebrating the downfall of the twin towers on the other side of the Hudson River that Tuesday morning (Kessler 2015).

Sinister Politics—The Birthers

Political CTs are of a different nature than many other kinds of CTs, as is discussed further in Chapter 5. Most often, they are calculated and spread from the top for political gain, i.e. these are bogus tales that are deliberately fabricated and spread for political benefits. Within this category, anti-Barack Obama CTs were, in effect, a separate grouping of their own, so abundant did they become leading up to, and during, his presidency between 2008 and 2016, as the first African American US head of state.

A relatively insignificant CT was sailing at full mast throughout his term: that he was not born in the USA and, thus, not legitimate as president. The story, without even any crumb of evidence, gained a surprising following on the right in American politics. In a 2010 poll conducted by the Pew Research Centre (2010), 18% of responders believed that the president was, indeed, a Muslim. Amongst Republicans this belief only grew stronger. This furthermore plays into the aforementioned CT that Muslims are secretly infiltrating the West, discussed further in Chapter 6. Implicating Obama in the plot, indicated, thus, that the conspiracy had already advanced to the very top levels of government.

These anti-Obama stories were not only being systematically spread from the top in an ominous plot. They were also bottom-up CTs. For example, on a conservative web portal in the USA, *Free Republic*, a contest was initiated by an anonymous poster called Jmouse007 in 2008. The contest was titled 'Pin the Middle Name on the Obama.' Barack Obama's middle name is Hussein, suggesting a Muslim heritage.

In a series of e-mails spread widely in the USA in 2007, it was not only insisted that Obama was a Muslim who had attended a radical Wahhabi school in Indonesia, but also that he had taken his oath of office for the US Senate by swearing on a Koran (Holan 2007). Never mind the well-established fact that Obama was a Christian and visibly took the oath of office on a Bible.

In one version, Obama was not only accused of being a Muslim, but also a communist. As was mentioned before, perhaps the most far-fetched story insisted that he was, in fact, the Antichrist (Posner 2008).

These anti-Obama CTs were not only being spread from the far-right, those suspicions were also used by his mainstream opponents for their own political gain. Even his fellow Democrat, Hillary Clinton, flirted with these tales for her potential political gain in the primaries before the 2008 US presidential elections.

By painting Obama as being *the other*, his opponents deliberately applied a Manichean method of demonising their adversary, a well-known tactic in populist politics, discussed further in Chapter 4.

Black—*And White*—Genocide

Related to religious CTs discussed earlier are, for example, those that centre on race. Amongst the most widespread of this kind of CT are, for instance, theories of a black genocide being underway. According to this CT, secret powerful actors of the white majority population are said to be operating a covert programme which has the deliberate aim of terminating African Americans in the USA. Presumably as a rhetorical tool, Malcolm X talked of a black genocide, while other leaders of blacks in America perhaps used it more literally. Taken as evidence of this black genocide already being in play was, for example, President Lyndon B. Johnson's plan of providing poor families with free birth control (Smith 1968).

As will be discussed later in the book there are, similarly, also those that insist a white genocide is being concocted. This includes the belief, amongst many white nationalists, that immigrants are flocking to predominantly white countries for the precise purpose of turning the white population into a minority within their own land, or even causing their extinction.

Rankings

Here, I have discussed some of the most widespread CTs in the public domain. When attempting to frame their range, many others can also be mentioned. For example, those that can be referred to as the tin-hat people, insisting that governments are intercepting human brains via satellites and secretly keeping surveillance of what their citizens are thinking—hence the tin hats to prevent the brain from being infiltrated. Another surprisingly widespread CT is that the US government had staged the 1969 moon-landing in a studio in Hollywood, presumably in order to advance the perceived position of the US in the Cold War vis-a-vis the Soviet Union.

The tales mentioned in this chapter are in no way a complete list of all the CTs out there. As has been discussed here, CTs come in various shapes and forms, which makes it difficult to place them into neat categories. In a study conducted by sampling a pool of Americans, Roland Imhoff and Pia Karoline Lamberty (2017) ranked 99 CTs that respondents believed in the most. The top ten on their list provide a good overview of common CTs. Ranking first, thus the most accepted and widespread theory on the list, was that George W. Bush had deliberately lied to get the US to invade Iraq; second, that John F. Kennedy was not killed by Lee Harvey Oswald acting alone; third, that Osama bin Laden had already long been dead when the US government claimed to have killed him; fourth, that the CIA was shipping prisoners to other countries to have them tortured; fifth, that revolutionary free energy technology was being suppressed by governments and the oil industry; sixth, that the USA was hiding UFO wreckage at the US Air Force facility in Nevada often referred to as Area 51; seventh, that it is only a matter of time before radio-frequency identification chips will be implemented in humans by authorities; eighth, that the Republicans used legal chicanery and fraud to win the 2000 US presidential election; ninth, that gun control is a tool to prevent the population from revolting against the government; and finally tenth, that Malcolm X was killed by government agents.

As can be seen here, these ten most accepted and widespread CTs in the study are of different types and range. Some might even be valid hypotheses, unveiling covert actions and bringing to light the real account of events, and thus do not really count as proper CTs. Parameters around what constitutes a proper CT are discussed further in the next chapter dealing with definitions.

Note

1. The John Birch Society is a radical-right advocacy group supporting limited government. It was founded by Robert W. Welch in 1958. The Birch Society was suspicious of various government activities and has upheld numerous conspiracy theories.

References

Abraham, L. (1973). *None dare call it conspiracy*. Seattle: The John Birch Society. Retrieved from digitalcollections.lib.washington.edu.
Akin, J. (2004, March 2). Meet Jack chick. *Catholic Answers Magazine*. El Cajon. catholic.com.

Arendt, J. (2014, February 19). The Illuminati purpose and plan for world takeover. Sayama: James Japan. Retrieved from jamesjpn.net.

Balmer, R. (2011, January 31). Billy Graham regrets political involvement, again. *Religion Dispatches*. Retrieved from religiondispatches.org.

Barkun, M. (2013). *A culture of conspiracy: Apocalyptic visions in contemporary America*. Berkeley: University of California Press.

Barruel. (2010 [1797]). *Memoirs illustrating the history of jacobinism: A translation from the French of the Abbe Barruel*. Berlin: Nabu Press.

Bilderberg mystery: Why do people believe in cabals? (2011, June 8). London. Bbc.com.

Bird, S. T., & Bogart, L. M. (2005). Conspiracy beliefs about HIV/AIDS and birth control among African Americans: Implications for the prevention of HIV, other STIs, and unintended pregnancy. *Journal of Social Issues, 61*(1), 109–126.

Boyer, P. (1994). *When time shall be no more: Prophecy belief in modern American culture*. Cambridge: Harvard University Press.

Brown, D. (2009). *The Da Vinci Code*. New York: Anchor.

Burns, J. F. (2008, November 8). In Diana inquest, a conspiracy theory with new twists. *The New York Times*. New York.

Bush, G. (1990, September 11). Address before a joint session of the Congress on the Persian Gulf crisis and the federal budget deficit. The American Presidency Project. Retrieved from presidency.ucsb.edu.

Byford, J. (2011). *Conspiracy theories: A critical introduction*. Basingstoke: Palgrave Macmillan.

Cooper, M. W. (1991). *Behold a pale horse*. Flagstaff: Light Technology Publishing.

Cooper, M. W. (2001, September 28). *Who benefits? The question no one dares to ask!* Retrieved from williamcooper.com.

De Poli, B. (2014). The Judeo-Masonic conspiracy: The path from the cemetery of Prague to Arab anti Zionist propaganda. In M. Butter & M. Reinkowski (Eds.), *Conspiracy theories in the United States and the Middle East*. Berlin: De Gruyter.

Dice, M. (2015). *The Bilderberg Group: Facts & fiction*. San Diego: The Resistance Manifesto.

Dulmen, R. V. (1992). *The society of the enlightenment*. Cambridge: St. Martin's Press.

Dyrendal, A. (2017). Conspiracy theory research in and about Norway. Unpublished COMPACT Cost action paper.

Fuller, R. C. (1996). *Naming the Antichrist: The history of an American obsession.* Oxford: Oxford University Press.

Griffin, D. (1976). *Fourth Reich of the rich.* Oxford: Emissary Publications.

Griffin, D. (2006). *9/11 and American empire: Intellectuals speak out* (Vol. 1). Northampton: Olive Branch Press.

Growing number of Americans Say Obama is a Muslim. (2010, August 18). Pew Research Center. Retrieved from pewforum.org.

Holan, A. D. (2007, December 20). *Obama used a Koran? No, he didn't.* Washington, DC. Politifact.com.

Hitler, A. (1925). *Mein Kampf* (People's ed.). Munich: Eher-Verlag.

Huxley, A. (1932). *Brave new world.* Toronto: Vintage Canada.

Imhof, R., & Lamberty, P. (2017). Too special to be duped: Need for uniqueness motivates conspiracy beliefs. *European Journal of Social Psychology., 47*(6), 724–734.

Jmouse007. (2008, February 29). *FR CONTEST: "Pin the middle name on the Obama."* Fresno: Free Republic. Retrieved from freerepublic.com.

Kalichman, S. (2009). *Denying AIDS: Conspiracy theories, pseudoscience, and human.* Göttingen: Copernicus—Springer.

Kessler, G. (2015, November 22). Trump's outrageous claim that 'thousands' of New Jersey Muslims celebrated the 9/11 attacks. *Washington Post.* Washington, DC.

Kyle, K. (2009). *Reporting the world.* New York: I. B. Tauris.

Levy, R. S., Bell, D. P., Donahue, W. C., Madigan, K., Morse, J., Shevitz, A. H., et al. (Eds.). (2005). *Antisemitism: A historical encyclopedia of prejudice and persecution.* Santa Barbara: ABC-CLIO.

Marsden, V. (2011 [1920]). *Protocols of the learned elders of Zion.* Austin: RiverCrest Publishing.

Miller, E. S. (2009). *Occult theocrasy.* CreateSpace [independent publishing platform].

Morse, S. F. B. (2007 [1835]). *Foreign conspiracy against the liberties of the United States: The numbers under the signature of Brutus.* Whitefish: Kessinger.

Popish Plot. (2017, November 12). *Encyclopedia Britannica.* Retrieved from britannica.com.

Porter, T. (2017, August 2). How the "deep state" conspiracy theory went mainstream. *Newsweek.* London.

Posner, S. (2008, October 27). Sarah posner: For many on the religious right, the prospect of an Obama presidency represents the end of life as we know it. *The Guardian.* London.

Potok, M., & Terry, D. (2015). *10 right-wing conspiracy theories that have slowly invaded American politics*. Salon. Retrieved from salon.com.

Robertson, P. (1991). *The new world order*. Dallas: W Publishing Group.

Robison, J. A. M. (1798). *Proofs of a conspiracy*. Appleton: Western Islands.

Ryan, K. (2017, August 27). *Sixteen more reasons to question 9/11*. [Blog] Retrieved from digwithin.net.

Sanburn, J. (2016). The world's most powerful and secret group, explained. *Time Magazine*. New York.

Schlafly, P. (1964). *A choice not an echo: The inside story of how American presidents are chosen*. Alton: Pere Marquette Press.

Scott, P. D. (2013). *The war conspiracy: JFK, 9/11, and the deep politics of war*. New York: Skyhorse.

Shermer, M., Grobman, A., & Hertzberg, A. (2009). *Denying history: Who says the holocaust never happened and why do they say it?* Berkeley: University of California Press.

Smith, M. (1968). *Birth control and the Negro woman*. Chicago: Johnson Publishing Company.

Webster, N. H. (1921). *World revolution: The plot against civilization*. London: Constable and Co Limited.

What is the "deep state"? (2017, March 9). London. TheEconomist.com.

Witchcraft and the Illuminati. (1999). CPA Books.

Wylie, J. A. (2002). *The papacy*. Brushton: TEACH Services.

Yardley, W. (2011, November 20). Oscar Ortega struggled with mental illness, family says. *The New York Times*. New York.

3

The Anatomy of Conspiracy Theories

The world is controlled by a Global Elite, a vast network of secret societies where the Illuminati stands at its core. Collectively, this hidden conglomerate can be referred to as the Brotherhood. It sits on top of a large pyramid dominating all spheres of human life: politics, finance, religion, education, military, intelligence agencies, drugs and organised crimes. You name it, the Brotherhood controls it. The administration of this secret world dominating force is complex but based on a clear hierarchy.

One of the most extensive and incongruous contemporary CTs out there is this grandiose discursive construction, build by British author David Icke—previously a BBC sports presenter—where most of the usual suspects and many other novel additions are weaved into one super CT explaining the entire world order and its design. Here, we find the most diverse and far-reaching gallery of actors and themes: the Rothschilds, the Bilderbergers, the Illuminati, the Vatican, etc. This sinister cabal operates, for example, a global reaching elite military, mind control activities, tax-exempt foundations, drugs and arms trade. Apparently, they also uphold evil political ideologies, such as capitalism, fascism, communism, Zionism, and religions such as Judaism and Islam (Barkun 2013).

© The Author(s) 2018
E. Bergmann, *Conspiracy & Populism*, https://doi.org/10.1007/978-3-319-90359-0_3

According to Icke, the world was being manipulated by these malevolent conspirators, who were preventing humanity from reaching its freedom and achieving its full potential. Natural progression was, thus, being halted by evil elements. As if that was not bad enough, Icke (1999) went on in later publications, to reveal that the Global Elite was, in turn, dominated by an extra-terrestrial authority called Draco. The Dracos, Icke claimed, were reptilians who only took on the appearance of humans. These humanoids not only existed on the surface of the planet like the rest of us, but, he explained, also lived deep inside the earth.

At the helm of the fantastically vast pyramid dominating life on earth, were those that he referred to as the Prison Warders. These were some sort of agents of what he called Luciferin Consciousness. In essence, these phenomena or creatures were the evil force in control of everything.

Tales of this bizarre discursive constellation have reached remarkably large audiences around the world. David Icke is a flamboyant character who travels the globe giving extensive lectures in huge auditoriums where he mixes New Age concepts, environmentalism and protection of Christianity into his message. Perhaps somewhat surprisingly, given the absurdity of the message, his large lecture halls are filled with people who seem genuinely interested in what he has to say.

After the 9/11 attacks in the USA, Icke (2002) immediately blamed the horrendous deed on the Illuminati and said that its aim was to trigger a nuclear war. He explained that the Illuminati would then exploit the tumult in its wake to seize control and instate their planned world government. He argued that the trauma of the terror would then allow the Brotherhood to implement their mind-control apparatus in the disguise of a counter terrorist tool. Icke included many, and mixed, explanations into his theory about 9/11. One aspect was that the conspirators had electronically taken over control of the planes remotely from the ground.

Despite how ludicrous his overall theory surely sounds to most ordinary ears, many of its elements have been adopted by not only other conspiracy theorists, but also by several prominent actors of the radical-right in politics. And, although Icke did not himself derive from the extreme Christian right, his creation was firmly being used by the far-right movement to advance their own message.

In this chapter, I explore the literature of CT studies and attempt to frame how they might be understood in the context of populist politics.

Conspiracies and Conspiracy Theories

Conspiracy theories have existed throughout history and seem to fulfil a human need of finding hidden designs and orchestrations underneath the chaos of our complex societies. Most generally, they denounce official accounts of events and, instead, unite in a common quest of explaining incidents and a state of affairs as products of covert plots of evil elites who, in secret, are systematically working to advancing their own narrow and often personal interests while harming the innocent and generally unknowing ordinary public.

In these stories, the conspiracy theorist is often placed as a heroic whistle-blower, standing alone between the pure public he is protecting and the evil elite who is exploiting the people and persecuting him.

The word conspiracy derives from Latin, *conspirare*, literally meaning to breathe together. It describes an act of two or more people, who are united in a quest for a commonly desired outcome (see Byford 2011). These are arrangements of a group of people who, in secret, cause harm to the public while advancing their own interest, usually either for economic or political gain. Proper real-life conspiracies are, of course, prevalent in human societies. Katherine K. Young and Paul Nathanson (2010) identify four features of every real conspiracy: first, they are coordinated acts of groups, 'not actions of isolated individuals'; second, they have 'illegal or sinister aims, not ones that would benefit society as a whole'; third, these are 'orchestrated acts, not a series of spontaneous and haphazard ones'; and fourth, they are plots made with 'secret planning, not public discussion.'

As Mark Fenster (1999) noted, while a conspiracy refers to an act, CTs refers to perception. Applied literarily, a CT, thus, covers the insistence of unravelling such a common covert action. In this context, CTs might surely be rational, the exploration into secret plots. History is full of generally dismissed conspiracies later proving to be true—for example, the Watergate scandal. Still, the term conspiracy theory is commonly only reserved for unproven explanations of malignant covert plots. Customarily, it is therefore not applied when discussing plausible explanations of clandestine plots. Furthermore, the term is typically limited to explanations of large scale or dramatic social and political events, such as the 9/11 attacks, distribution of AIDS, the death of Diana or of the Bilderbergers ruling the world.

In this book, we are thus not dealing with conspiracies as such. Accounts of proven conspiracies such as the Iran-Contra affair or former and more mysterious conspiracies like the Dreyfus affair in France are therefore not of specific interest here—however interesting they otherwise might be. These conspiracies and many more like them that have been uncovered over the years are now considered topics of mainstream historical analysis and, thus, do not count as CTs in the way they are understood here. Neither are we, here, dealing with plausible rival hypotheses to official accounts, such as the US government hiding or fabricating evidence to facilitate the Iraq invasion.

Instead, CTs are understood here as a whole other species. Rather, they are unprovable counter cultural claims that contradict conventional accounts of events. Here, we are thus entering into a field of explanations that overreach legitimate hypotheses of conspiratorial actions.

Stigmatized Knowledge

In this understanding, the term conspiracy theory is far from being a neutral analytical concept. As mentioned in the introduction to this book, it is a pejorative label slapped on other people's explanations that are perceived to be bogus. People usually don't refer to themselves as conspiracy theorists. In effect, the term is an insult.

This is what Michael Barkun (2013) refers to when describing CTs as stigmatised knowledge, i.e. knowledge that has not (at least yet) received the stamp of approval by mainstream institutions. As such, the label is a tool used to delegitimize rival explanations. In fact, as Tim Aistrope (2016) argues, the term has effectively been brandished as a discursive weapon to cast others as not credible. In this regard, he argues that the USA has, for example, systematically applied the label in its foreign policy for discrediting purposes, to cast aspersions on rival explanations of their own actions as unfounded.

Michael Butter and Peter Knight (2016) point out that CTs almost inevitably entail stigmatized knowledge. They claim that CTs are distinguishable from other explanations of events by the 'particular content and social function of the story that is told in opposition to received wisdom.' By slapping the label on one's opponents, the proponent of an alternative account of events is denigrated as being paranoid, irrational and delusional. The counterclaim can thus, without much proper examination, be dismissed as merely being a CT, and, therefore, not valid as a credible hypothesis.

Divisions and Categories

As was established in the previous chapter, CTs are of various kinds and range, reaching from unravelling only isolated plots—such as who killed Kennedy—to describing the entirety of human order in contemporary times as well as in history. To understand the nature of different CTs, it is therefore necessary to separate them into different categories. Michael Barkun (2013) offers one such systemic categorisation, separating three types, distinguished primarily by scope and ranked in ascending order of breadth.

One category covers CTs offering alternative explanations of certain isolated events, such as of the 9/11 attacks, death of Princess Diana and the deliberate spread of the Aids virus. A second category is framed around those that aim to unravel vast conspiratorial systems, such as of evil forces seizing control over peoples and countries, or of infiltrating and subverting institutions and societies. Amongst such kinds of CTs are, for example, plots of Zionist world domination, CTs surrounding the Bilderberg group and more recently the so-called Eurabia theory, the fear of an Islamist takeover in Europe—discussed further in Chapter 6.

In the third category are theories of super-conspiracies, overall conspiratorial constructs in which multiple conspiracies are seen to be linked together hierarchically. These are complex conglomerates, upheld by authors like David Icke discussed at the beginning of this chapter, in which both event-based and systemic CTs are intertwined into a single overall theory. This category thus covers theories insisting that almost the entire world order can be explained through actions of a distant but all-powerful evil force.

In the literature on CTs, several other distinctions have been offered. Jesse Walker (2013), for example, grounds his distinction mainly on where in the story the enemy is based. First on his list are CTs in which the enemy is placed on the outside; these are tales of devilish external actors threatening the community. These CTs are, for example, upheld by right-wing populists—including the Eurabia theory. Secondly, Walker identifies CTs placing enemies within society, for example, those identifying Zionist plots from within.

Third on his list are CTs unmasking enemies above: these are tales of powerful people exploiting the ordinary people for their own sinister gain. These can, for example, be stories of corrupt domestic elites betraying the public. The fourth category places the enemy below in society, suspicions of subgroups undermining the community. Previously, these were often workers or ethnic groups such as, for example, Roma people. Now, these stories often revolve around qualms about foreign immigrants in Western societies. The fifth and last category on Walker's list are, contrary to the previous kinds, theories of benevolent conspiracies, i.e. of forces for good working behind the scenes in order to improve societies. They deviate from those more commonly upheld, where the aim is to unmask an enemy of the people.

Practical or Pathological Paranoia

As can be seen here, CTs are of various kinds. And while CTs have for decades and even centuries been widely discussed in media and literature, rigid academic analysis of CTs is relatively recent. As was mentioned in the introduction chapter, Historian Richard Hofstadter's (1964) essay, *The Paranoid Style in American Politics*, is generally considered to be the first contemporary scholarly attempt of systematically understanding the role CTs play in Western societies. It was first introduced in the wake of the Kennedy assassination in 1963 and published in its final form in 1965.

Hofstadter viewed those that were prone to subscribe to CTs as harmful deviants in human societies, delusional people who, by undermining necessary trust in public institutions, were ripping apart the fabric of our societies. Hofstadter, and many other scholars studying the field in the early years, tended to view CTs as a kind of mental illness, metaphorically describing those that upheld them as being pathological and paranoid. And although Hofstadter mainly used the term paranoid as a metaphor, rather than literal, he still firmly viewed conspiracy theorists as dangerous deviants on the periphery of society. These, he said, were radical activists who based their politics on a paranoid fear fueled by conspiracies.

In this regard, CTs are almost automatically met with scepticism and distain. In this understanding, they are seen as a menace to society and the actions of authorities, thus, are aimed at repressing these unwanted kinds of explanations. As pathologized in this manner, CTs are, thus, by definition always wrong.

Later, many scholars came to criticise this view. Around the millennium, numerous books were being published countering this psycho-historical and pathologizing view.

Mark Fenster (1999) was one of the first to move away from the focus on paranoia and treated CTs instead as a populist theory of power, an expression of populist protest. In this way, Fenster recognises that CTs can function as a tool of the weaker groups in society, an expression against inequality and powerlessness. Here, CTs are seen as a symptom of actual political and social conditions. Just because CTs might be wrong, he wrote, 'does not mean that they are not on to something.'

Thus, rather than dismissing them outright as being paranoid and pathological, CTs might instead be viewed as a form of radical populist discourse, where a secret elite is perceived to be manipulating economic, political and social relations.

Similarly, Peter Knight (2001) argues that CTs cannot only be dismissed as delusional ranting of the fringe elements in society, but that they rather constitute 'many people's normal way of thinking about who they are and how the world works.' Knight maintains that CTs reflect a sceptical view of governmental authority and official versions of events. This is not far from Fenster's view, in which CTs seem to function as a form of populist discourse, often quite radical. In doing so, Fenster maintains that CTs need to be seen as symptoms of actual political and social conditions. As is discussed in following chapters, this applies equally when analysing right-wing populism.

Furthermore, Michael Barkun (2013) maintains that a conspiracy belief is in itself neither necessarily determinative of paranoia nor divorced from it. Instead, he wrote, 'conspiracism straddles a blurred and shifting boundary between pathology and normalcy.'

Clare Birchall (2006) moves even closer towards legitimising CTs when claiming that they are far more common amongst the general public than many scholars acknowledge. She thus attributes certain legitimacy and even practicality to CTs when maintaining that they provide a 'form of popular knowledge or interpretation' of events or the state of affairs.

On a similar note, Michael Butter (2014) argues against conspiracy theories being marginalised, as they are indeed widespread and influential.

Philosopher Matthew Dentith (2014) finds that in some circumstances, a belief in CTs can indeed be rational. On these grounds, he denounces definitions that cast those that believe in them as always being irrational and, as a result, in the wrong. Rather, he defines a CT much more broadly, as 'any explanation of an event that cites a conspiracy as a salient cause.' He says that ruling out a conspiracy from the outset, in itself, eschews any investigation into events away from that possibility. That would be similar to ruling out surprise parties, Dentith wrote, and perhaps much of office politics. In this understanding, CTs are not a mental illness. Rather, he maintains, it is a sign of health to be suspicious of Machiavellian secret plots, as history is indeed full of opaque acts of secret groups.

These scholars all argue that CTs are not necessarily always bogus and upheld only by the delusional. Indeed, CTs should be taken seriously as part of contemporary culture. Although they might be flawed and impossible to prove, CTs should neither be dismissed out of hand as they might, indeed, hold some truth to them. However, although we might agree that CTs are not necessarily always a sign of irrational paranoia, they are not usually the most probable explanation of events or a state of affairs. As Uscinski et al. (2016) point out, CTs are most often based on unprovable mistrusts and myths. Here, Joseph Heller (1961) in the phrase from his novel *Catch-22* might perhaps be helpful: 'Just because you're paranoid doesn't mean they aren't after you.'

Design

As has been established here, CTs are not only of several kinds and can be classified according to different criteria, they are also understood in a variety of ways. Framing what they collectively constitute can, thus, be quite a complex task. Essentially, though, CTs attempt to make sense of the world often by tying together seemingly unrelated events.

They can, thus, be seen as a separate rhetorical style of explaining social and political events. As was discussed in the introduction to this book, they are in their own way a specific tradition of explanation. As a story telling style, they often hold remarkably similar structures and internal explanatory logic. In addition to the common belief that hidden powerful actors control human acts, they are often incredibly detailed and complex and tend to offer a simplistic vision of antagonism between the *people* and the *elites*. In other words, CTs can be seen as a distinctive culture of a conspicuous world view: a separate system of style, values, beliefs and knowledge (Byford 2011).

A common feature of the vast flora of CTs is presenting an alternative narrative to established knowledge. In other words, for them to exist there must, thus, be an official accepted account to contradict.

Another common trope is viewing social or political events as a consequence of a carefully worked out covert plan of powerful actors for their own gain, to the detriment of the general public. Insisting that behind the façade of the seeming reality of society are powerful actors plotting in secret for advancing their own gain against the interest of the many. In other words, the visible reality is an illusion. Thus, in addition to secret evil deeds, CTs usually also insist that the generally accepted account is not only false but based on active deception. Most often, the story involves a smokescreen that is being installed in order to hide the truth (Imhof and Lamberty 2016).

Within these parameters, Michael Barkun (2013) describes the conspiratorial worldview as seeing the universe being 'governed by design rather than by randomness.' Here, history is viewed as 'controlled by massive demonic forces' and furthermore that 'powerful, hidden, evil forces control human destinies.' Collectively, he identifies the following three common features: Nothing happens by accident; nothing is as it seems; and everything is connected. In other words, everything is seen to be designed to precision.

At its core, CTs thus claim to uncover the real power relationships in the world. Along those lines, Bartlett and Miller (2010) define CTs as being an 'account of events as the deliberate product of powerful few, regardless of the evidence.' This last element of disregarding evidence brings forth the next aspect of discussion; we are dealing with non-falsifiable truths.

Unverifiable Truths

Michael Barkun (2013) explains how CTs can be difficult to dismiss as conspiracy theorists tend to incorporate whatever evidence is offered to denounce them, so that they often become a closed system of unverifiable truths, and, as such, ultimately become much rather a 'matter of faith than proof.'

Empirical hypothesis is separated from, for example, religious belief by being testable. This is what separates science from faith. And although CTs often claim to be empirical hypotheses, they tend not to be testable. The evidence offered is often only disguised as testable data. These can be sweeping explanations of vast events with complex and often contradictory testimony. Those highly complex social constructions are then habitually explained as resulting from very simple causes. Human affairs are then seen through that same prism.

This element can make CTs difficult to analyse. Barkun (2013) for example discusses how all evidence against the theory tends to be dismissed as false and explained away by insisting that the powerful conspirators are in control of the spread of information and, thus, in a position of fabricating false evidence to mislead those that seek to expose the conspiracy. If someone finds out the truth, the conspirators take to discrediting the whistle-blower.

Conspiracy theorists, thus, defeat any attempt of testing by explaining how the examiners, whether they are in the media, academia or politics, are all in on the plot. In other words, regardless of the evidence, events are nonetheless seen as a result of concealed actions of evil-doers. As a result, the theory becomes non-falsifiable (ibid.).

Conspiracy theories therefore tend to become a closed explanatory system. And although they might have grains of truth in them, their problem lies in a lack of provability. In essence, these are counter-truths that cannot be verified. All evil deeds and mysteries, such as diseases, addictions and deaths, in addition to who is awarded what in life, outcome of sports games, and other human affairs can be seen as part of the plot. It's all a conspiracy. And as CTs are unprovable they become the perfect ingredient for fake news stories, distributed online, as is discussed in Chapter 7.

Secrecy and Agency

Secrecy is firmly intertwined into any proper CT. These are stories of plots of powerful people hatched out in secret, covert acts are thus always in play. Without secrecy, it's not a CT. Barkun (2013) differentiates between secrets of groups and secret of actions. According to him, CTs can claim to unravel two main types of secrecy: First, there are secret acts of secret groups, such as the Illuminati. Secondly, there are secret acts of known groups, such as of the Bilderbergers, Freemasons, the CIA, etc. Usually there also must be elements of mystery to unravel, preferably a complex web of deception.

As has also been established here, another core ingredient of CTs is intentionality, which is always built into the story. CTs insist on intentions. Things occur because someone wills them to occur, not because of randomness or accident. In other words, the social order is a result of intentional plots of hidden malignant powerful actors. Agency is a key component. These are not critical analyses of structural systems evolving over time through a variety of interactions and without a firm intent of identifiable and usually only few actors.

As Jamie Bartlett and Carl Miller (2010) show, it can, though, be difficult to distinguish between a CT and a well-structured account of events, for example, revealing structures that favour the powerful few to the detriment of the larger public. Marxist critical theory, for instance, analyses the structural setup of the capitalist order, which is seen as being biased against the poor and the powerless and in favour of the powerful few. As was discussed in Chapter 1, it is thus not always easy to separate between a critical theory of the capitalist order and outright CTs.

Timothy Melley (2000) argues that while CTs 'articulate a critique of powerful institutions,' they depart from progressive analysis by 'substituting simplistic populist vision of antagonism between "the people" and "the elites" for a truly detailed analysis of complex power structures.'

Many scholars of critical theory maintain that financiers, international bankers, and multinational institutions unite in constructing and upholding a system benefitting the rich and exploiting the poor. This, though, is not a proper CT as it lacks the agency of a true covert group of few powerful actors. However, maintaining that the capitalist order is controlled by groups like the Bilderbers, moves away from conventional critical structural analysis and into the field of CTs. Thus, what sets CTs apart from critical theory is the insistence on continuous secret agency and intention.

However, we also must note that examples of real-life conspiracies are of course, ample, both in history and in contemporary society. Critical investigations into possible conspiracies can thus play an important role in democratic society, as they can indeed help in bringing misdeeds into light. We must, thus, distinguish between plausible and utterly bogus CTs—here we are mainly dealing with the latter.

Good and Evil

At their very core, CTs claim to uncover secret plots hatched out by evil elites. They entail the insistence that the world is controlled by dominating demonic forces. Like populists—who are discussed in the following chapter—conspiracy theorists thus tend to separate between *good* and *evil*. This is similar to both religion and populist accounts of political affairs (Hawkins 2003). Both strands discussed here, populism and CTs, can, thus, be characterised as being *Manichean*, offering a binary world view of a struggle between light and darkness.

The in-group is commonly positioned as a victim of the powerful out-group, who is accused of being implicated in morally questionable actions.

As has been discussed here, CTs revolve around plots of both secret and malignant forces. We are, in other words, dealing with tales of actions of evildoers. Usually, conspiracy theorists attempt to awaken the public, encouraging them to face their oppressors or manipulators. Thus, correspondingly to populists, conspiracy theorists discursively create an *Other*, an enemy of the people. Those opposing their claim are then simply cast as agents of the conspirators and in that way delegitimised.

Michael Barkun (2013) distinguishes between conspiracy theorists and millennialism. He points out that although CTs, like millenialists, locate and describe evil, they do not offer explanations for its defeat. Thus, although CTs offer a binary world view of a struggle between good and evil, they depart from, for example, religion by not always predicting that good will necessarily prevail over evil and they do not, in itself, advocate a millennialist or utopian outlook for the future.

Next, I discuss the appeal of CTs before turning to discuss the people who believe in them.

Making Sense

In the fast-changing, globalised, high-tech world, the simplicity promised by CTs can become alluring. Indeed, one of the main appeals of CTs is in offering a simplistic dualistic re-enchantment of the world (Giry 2017). Casting the world order as being a result of evil deeds of elites against the ordinary man reduces highly complex social problems down to often a simple single answer. Cognitively, this can be quite comforting.

In this regard, endorsement of CTs can be seen as epistmetic, i.e. based on a very human desire of understanding and making sense of one's social environment. Conspiratorialism, thus, in essence, revolves around finding meaning in a social order, which otherwise appears to be random. In other words, the main attraction of CTs is in making sense of a chaotic world.

Along those lines, Crystal Park (2010) for example, concluded that when feeling anxious and uncertain, people cognitively seek to find patterns and hidden meaning in order to make sense of the world. When feeling powerless and deprived, CTs can, she maintained, be applied to blame others for one's own misfortune.

More systematically, Barkun (2013) identifies three main appeals of CTs: First, they claim to explain what institutional analysis cannot; secondly, most often, they offer a simple view by sharp distinction between *light* and *darkness*, between good and evil; and, thirdly, they offer new secret knowledge unknown to others.

Another function of CTs is in validating the in-group as competent and moral, while under threat from unscrupulous others. These evil others can then, in turn, be blamed for ill-fates of the defined in-group (Douglas et al. 2017).

Subscribing to a CT can bring comfort and a separate identity for the believer. Conspiratorialism can indeed become a lifestyle in and of its own. As Daniel Pipes (1999) put it; 'a way of seeing life itself.' This becomes the prism thorough which the world is seen, effectively streamlining reality in an effort to make sense out of a chaotic world. Effectively, CTs become like a sort of secular religion. Believing in an ordered universe turns into a matter of faith, rather than being based on any sort of conventional proof (Barkun 2013).

As has already been discussed here, CTs can be seen as stigmatised knowledge. These are opinions that have not been accepted by the mainstream. The conspiracy theorist is thus marginalised or even ridiculed. Upholding CTs can thus bring with it a personal stigma. The flip side to that can, however, also be seen as a functional benefit for the theorist, the insistence of knowing what others don't know.

Studies have shown that those who endorse CTs often have a need for being unique and, thus, wish to stand out from the crowd (Imhof and Lamberty 2016). Endorsing a CT might compensate for the notion of not being in control. It can feel empowering to be the one seeing through the smoke screens, being the one that is not afraid of speaking truth to power. This can embolden a sense of being special, if being able to see a truth that is hidden to others.

For Losers?

There is still no consensus as to what brings some people to have a belief in CTs while others do not. The literature exploring the causes behind conspiratorialism has hitherto mainly been dominated by scholars of social psychology. Most often, they have been preoccupied with investigating deviance (Butter and Knight 2016). Key explanatory terms have, for instance, included uncertanty, unsecurity, anxiety, distess, sense-making, powerlessness, lack of control, social conflict and victemhood. In some cases, social psychologists have also associated belief in CTs with belief in paranormal activities, such as magnetism and other supernatural aspects.

Karen Douglas et al. (2017) found that conspiratorialism correlates with a lack of socio-political control. Those who have an increased need for preserving their beliefs in the face of uncertainty and contradiction were found to be more likely than others to endorse CTs. Belief in CTs thus compensates for the lack of feeing able to control outcomes that affects one's social environment. The study also showed that distress can as well bring people to have a belief in CTs. This plays directly into peoples' need to feel safe. Douglas and her colleagues thus argue that when these needs are threatened, people become more likely to turn to CTs for comfort.

Here, another finding of Uscinski et al. (2016) is relevant. Their study showed that unfulfilled political ambitions can lead people to endorse CTs. Just as with other kinds of misfortunes, it can be soothing to explain them away by pointing to a malignant plot of external actors and, thus, absolve oneself from any responsibility over the unfavourable situation.

In this regard, CTs can be seen here as a form of refuge of the powerless. They are often more widespread in isolated societies and amongst those that are socially excluded. Ted Goertzel (1994), for example, found that those of a minority status, such as African Americans and Latinos, were more likely to believe in CTs. Although still being contested in the literature, many studies have indicated that conspiracy beliefs decrease with the attainment of higher education (van Prooijen 2016). Studies have furthermore indicated that belief in CTs correlates with diminished analytical thinking (Douglas et al. 2017).

In a more stigmatising manner, Joe Uscinski and Joe Parent (2014) concluded that CTs are 'for losers,' for those that have lost out in life. They found that conspiracy beliefs were higher amongst those that had lost out in the contemporary fast changing society or felt threatened by political processes.

Here, the feeling of being under-privileged, or a victim of social processes, was found to enhance beliefs in CTs. These conclusions were, for example, supported by Imhoff and Bruder (2014). They furthermore found that those who tended to attribute their misfortune to the actions of others were more likely to be mistrustful and paranoid and, as a result, increasingly prone to foster a belief in CTs.

Predispositions

Scholars have long debated whether those on the political left or right are more likely to endorse CTs. Recently, high profile CTs have flourished within groups on the radical-right, as will be discussed further in following chapters. This has led many to hypothesise that the political far-right is perhaps more susceptible to CTs. Still, however, the only linear relationship persistently found in most studies is between extremism as such, and endorsing CTs, in general. Those further out on the periphery of the political spectrum have consistently been found more likely to promote CTs than those closer to centre. Bartlett and Miller (2010), for example, found that most extremist groups applied CTs rigorously in their rhetoric.

In other words, those on the radical-left and extreme-right were found to be equally conspiratorial minded. Both extremes have a similar tendency to propagate CTs to a much greater extent than those of the mainstream (Pipes 1999).

Partisan attachment has, in many studies, consistently been found to predict political opinions. This also applies to CTs. In their study exploring the causes behind conspiratorial beliefs, Uscinski et al. (2016) concluded that there exists a unique predisposition that drives those who associate strongly with a partisan attachment to believing in CTs. Endorsing specific CTs is closely linked to partisanship. Prior political inclinations are, in other words, a decisive factor in determining what CTs people might uphold. Or perhaps rather, the way information and predispositions are entangled has a decisive impact on what people might believe.

Similarly, like any other opinions people might hold, CTs are thus, also subject to confirmation bias. We all tend to look for factors that support our own beliefs, often while automatically dismissing other information as unfounded—presumably even without noticing it. This shields our worldview from invalidation. Now, of course, information affects our beliefs, but—and this is the main point here—it is, however, not irrespective of our prior disposition. We tend to interpret information to fit our prior beliefs.

Generally, we are, as a result, much more likely to suspect people belonging to other political factions of covert malignant plots than we are to suspect those within our own camp. In this regard, it is perhaps not surprising that those on the left were more inclined to think that US Republican President George W. Bush was in on the 9/11 attacks, while those on the right disproportionally insisted that his successor from the opposite side, Barack Obama, was foreign born.

However, although predisposition can determine which CTs we are more likely to endorse, it does not explain why certain individuals of each side are more likely to believe in them. Although Democrats are more likely than Republicans to suspect George W. Bush of being involved in the 9/11 attacks, most Democrats still don't believe any of that. Similarly, even though Birthers tend to be Republicans, not all Republicans are Birthers.

Conspiratorial Correlations

One of the most strongly correlated relations found in these studies exploring causes behind conspiratorial thinking shows that people who believe in one CT are more likely to believe in others. Conspiracy theorists are, thus, likely to believe in a variety of CTs. Quite often, they believe in theories that contradict each other, even those that by all conventional rationalisations are mutually exclusive. For example, a study in 2012 found that people who believe that Osama Bin Laden was captured alive by the US army were also more likely to believe that he had long been dead when the USA claimed to have killed him in 2011 (Wood et al. 2012).

Another interesting finding of these studies investigating conspiratorial thinking is that people were more likely to believe in a conspiracy around major events when consequences were severe and distressing (van Prooijen and van Dijk 2014). Small-scale mundane explanations can feel unsatisfying around large-scale events (Douglas et al. 2017). Not only do CTs often provide more interesting explanations to events, but sometimes they are also more proportional to fit their scale—as they are indeed built around what they aim to explain.

Furthermore, people are more likely to suspect successful acts of being a result of a conspiracy rather than attempts that fail. Unsuccessful assassination attempts against a president are, for example, less likely to spur conspiracy suspicions than when a leader is actually killed. This can be irrespective of evidence, i.e. even though the evidence might suggest otherwise, the success of the alleged conspiracy is taken to prove that there was one.

Yet another study found that highly Machiavellian people were more likely to belief in CTs, as they themselves were more inclined to engage in conspiracies (Douglas and Sutton 2011). Wall street traders were, for example, found to be amongst the most conspiracy minded. Similar results were found amongst people in politics and journalism. Many media reports obviously start out from investigating a CT.

General and Widespread

Probably because of their outlandishness, scholars have tended to treat belief in CTs as a unique species of opinion (Uscinski et al. 2016). As a result, conspiracy theorists have often been regarded as being psychologically troubled; some sort of misfits in society. Especially within the field of social psychology, scholars have tended to apply clinical terms to them describing paranoia and delusion when exploring potential causes.

However, countering the view amongst many social psychologists who maintain that endorsing CTs points to being on the fringes of society, many CTs have proven to be surprisingly widespread. For example, in surveys continuously sampled by Oliver and Wood (2016), a majority of Americans respondents consistently agreed with at least one commonly held CT. More than half, for instance, don't accept the official version that President John F. Kennedy was assassinated by Lee Harvey Oswald acting alone.

A quarter of US citizens furthermore believe Barack Obama was foreign born (Uscinski et al. 2016); a third dismiss global warming as a hoax (Douglas et al. 2017) and up to half suspect authorities of hiding information about UFOs (Byford 2011).

Surveys show that between 30 and 40% of people in the USA don't believe the official accounts of the 9/11 attacks (Byford 2011). In other words, around a third of the population suspects the government of either being involved in a cover up or even themselves being in on the horrendous act. This so-called *Truther* movement has only a little less support in Europe.

In the UK, significant number of people don't buy official explanations surrounding the death of Princess Diana.

Taking into account that a diverse range of people do seem to endorse varieties of CTs, it seems quite futile to dismiss them all as delusional. Thus, how prominent and widespread many CTs have become contradicts the notion that believing in them first and foremost indicates a personality disorder. Michael Billig (1978) warned that it is 'easy to overemphasise its eccentricities at the expense of noticing what is psychologically commonplace.'

Conspiratorial thinking has, in fact, gone democratically mainstream. Explaining the existence of CTs can, thus, not merely be limited to individual cognitive biases, crippled epistemology or social abnormality. Conspiracies do occur and it can, thus, quite simply, often be sensible to believe in them.

Accordingly, conspiratorialism has recently been transmitted into mainstream culture on both sides of the Atlantic, in novels, movies and television series. Recent years have also seen an avalanche of mainstream non-fiction literature discussing conspiracies in a variety of ways and forms.

I mentioned before that one of the functional benefits some individuals might reap from upholding CTs is in standing out of the crowd, of being the one seeing through all the deception. The recent popularity of CTs in mainstream culture might, thus, deprive them of some of their allure; that is, of being amongst only very few in the know, and, as a result, drive some conspiracy theorists into even deeper and more dramatic discoveries.

Precariousness

Although people who are prone to endorse CTs have, in surveys and experiments, tended to share some specific attributes, the spread of these tales are often much more prevalent than can easily be ascribed to only fringe elements in society. As has firmly been established here, endorsing CTs is in no way limited only to people with some sort of personality disorder.

Still, conspiratorial thinking is not merely reminiscent of just any other belief system, such as religion or political inclinations. Surely, fanciful concocted tales of conspiracies can be amusing, but they can also be precarious. Not only because they might disrupt trust in public institutions and democratic systems, but also by dint of driving some of their more unstable subscribers to violent actions—such as Anders Breivik, discussed at the beginning of this book.

Karen Douglas (2017), for instance, found that being presented with unsubstantiated material of covert plots around the death of Princess Diana made respondents in their study become more likely to suspect misconduct. This occurred without the participants in the experiment even realising their own change of mind. The study also found that exposure to CTs left participants feeling uncertain and disillusioned.

Studies conducted by Uscinski and Parent (2014) indicate that conspiratorial thinking can lead to anti-social behaviour. Jolley and Douglas (2014) furthermore established that those who are suspicious of science were, for example, less likely to seek medical care and more prone to practise risky sexual behaviour. They were also more likely to hold racist sentiments and less committed to human rights and civil liberties.

Douglas and Sutton (2008) found that CTs can have hidden impacts. Their study showed, for example, that being exposed to CTs can alter people's political attitudes, even without them being aware of it. Similarly, Bartlett and Miller (2010) insist that there is a clear correlation between extremism and belief in CTs. They concluded that CTs serve as what they coin as being a 'radicalising multiplier.' In other words, being exposed to CTs can lead those more susceptible to them to turn to political extremism.

Finally, Wood et al. (2012) showed that once a person has taken on a belief in misinformation, it can prove difficult to erode that creed. It can, in other words, be a daunting task, that of convincing people that they have adopted a wrong view about the world.

References

Aistrope, T. (2016). *Conspiracy theory and American foreign policy*. Manchester: Manchester University Press.

Barkun, M. (2013). *A culture of conspiracy: Apocalyptic visions in contemporary America*. Berkeley: University of California Press.

Bartlett, J., & Miller, C. (2010). *The power of unreason: Conspiracy theories, extremism and counter-terrorism*. London: Demos. Retrieved from westernvoice.net.

Billig, M. (1978). *Fascists: A social psychological view of the National Front*. London: Academic Press.

Birchall, C. (2006). *Knowledge goes pop: From conspiracy theory to gossip*. Oxford: Berg Publishers.

Butter, M. (2014). *Plots, designs, and schemes: American conspiracy theories from the Puritans to the present*. Berlin: De Gruyter.

Butter, M., & Knight, P. (2016). Bridging the great divide: Conspiracy theory research for the 21st century. *Diogenes*. https://doi.org/10.1177/0392192116669289.

Byford, J. (2011). *Conspiracy theories: A critical introduction*. Basingstoke: Palgrave Macmillan.

Dentith, M. (2014). *The philosophy of conspiracy theories*. Basingstoke: Palgrave Macmillan.

Douglas, K. (2017). *You just can't trust 'em: Conspiracy theories erode peoples faith in politicians and democracy itself.* Brussels: International Politics and Society. Retrieved from ips-journal.eu.

Douglas, K., & Sutton, R. (2008). The hidden impact of conspiracy theories: Perceived and actual influence of theories surrounding the death of Princess Diana. *The Journal of Social Psychology, 148*(2), 210–222.

Douglas, K., & Sutton, R. (2011). Does it take one to know one? Endorsement of conspiracy theories is influenced by personal willingness to conspire. *British Journal of Social Psychology, 50*(3), 544–552.

Douglas, K., Sutton, R., & Cichocka, A. (2017). The psychology of conspiracy theories. *Current Directions in Psychological Science, 26*, 538–542. https://doi.org/10.1177/0963721417718261.

Fenster, M. (1999). *Conspiracy theories: Secrecy and power in American culture.* Minneapolis: University of Minnesota Press.

Giry, J. (2017). *A functionalist analysis of conspiracy theories: Conspiracy theories and their social functions.* Unpublished paper retrieved from academia.edu.

Goertzel, T. (1994). Belief in conspiracy theories. *Political Psychology, 15*(4), 731–742.

Hawkins, K. (2003). Populism in Venezuela: The rise of Chavismo. *Third World Quarterly, 24*(6), 1137–1160.

Heller, J. (1961). *Catch 22.* Munchen: Simon & Schuster.

Hofstadter, R. (1964). *The paranoid style in American politics.* New York: Vintage Books.

Icke, D. (1999). *The biggest secret: The book that will change the world.* Wildwood: Bridge of Love Publication.

Icke, D. (2002). *Alice in Wonderland and the World Trade Center disaster.* Wildwood: Bridge of Love Publication.

Imhoff, R., & Bruder, M. (2014). Speaking (un-)truth to power: Conspiracy mentality as a generalised political attitude. *European Journal of Personality, 28*(1), 25–43. https://doi.org/10.1002/per.1930.

Imhof, R., & Lamberty, P. (2016). Too special to be duped: Need for uniqueness motivates conspiracy beliefs. *European Journal of Social Psychology, 47*(6), 724–734. https://doi.org/10.1002/ejsp.2265.

Jolley, D., & Douglas, K. M. (2014). The social consequences of conspiracism: Exposure to conspiracy theories decreases intentions to engage in politics and to reduce one's carbon footprint. *British Journal of Psychology, 105*(1), 35–56. https://doi.org/10.1111/bjop.12018.

Knight, P. (2001). *Conspiracy culture: From the Kennedy assassination to the X-Files*. Abingdon-on-Thames: Routledge.

Melley, T. (2000). *Empire of conspiracy: The culture of paranoia in postwar America*. Ithaca: Cornell University Press.

Oliver, J. E. (2016). Rise of the Trumpenvolk: Populism in the 2016 election. *The ANNALS of the American Academy of Political and Social Science, 667*(1), 189–206.

Park, C. L. (2010). Making sense of the meaning literature: An integrative review of meaning making and its effects on adjustment to stressful life events. *Psychological Bulletin, 136*(2), 257.

Pipes, D. (1999). *Conspiracy: How the paranoid style flourishes and where it comes from*. New York: Simon & Schuster.

van Prooijen, J. -W. (2016). Sometimes inclusion breeds suspicion: Self-uncertainty and belongingness predict belief in conspiracy theories. *European Journal of Social Psychology, 46*(3), 267–279.

van Prooijen, J. -W., & van Dijk, E. (2014). When consequence size predicts belief in conspiracy theories: The moderating role of perspective taking. *Journal of Experimental Social Psychology, 55*, 63–73.

Uscinski, J. E., & Parent, J. M. (2014). *American conspiracy theories*. Oxford: Oxford University Press.

Uscinski, J. E., Klofstad, C., & Atkinson, M. D. (2016). What drives conspiratorial beliefs? The role of informational cues and predispositions. *Political Research Quarterly, 69*(1), 57–71.

Walker, J. (2013). *The United States of paranoia: A conspiracy theory*. New York: Harper.

Wood, M. J., Douglas, K. M., & Sutton, R. M. (2012). Dead and alive: Beliefs in contradictory conspiracy theories. *Social Psychological and Personality Science, 3*(6), 767–773.

Young, K. K., & Nathanson, P. (2010). *Sanctifying misandry: Goddess ideology and the fall of man*. Ithaca: McGill-Queen's University Press.

4

Dissecting Populism

On 19 April 1995, a 27-year-old US Army veteran from Lockport, New York parked his rented van in front of the Federal Building in Oklahoma City and detonated an ammonium nitrate fertilizer and nitromethane bomb. The attack, commonly referred to as the Oklahoma City bombing, killed 168 people and injured hundreds more. Timothy McVeigh committed the domestic grown terrorist attack in revenge of the federal government's handling of the Waco siege in Texas in 1993 where 76 followers of the Christian sect, the Branch Davidians, died, including their leader, David Koresh.

McVeigh came to believe in a series of anti-government CTs and visited, for example, Area 51, where he believed the government was hiding evidence of UFOs. In a letter to his childhood friend, Steve Hodge, prior to his action, he pledged his allegiance to the Constitution of the USA and accused the government of having betrayed the founding fathers, and that it should be punished accordingly. He wrote: 'I have come to peace with myself, my God and my cause. Blood will flow in the streets, Steve. Good vs. Evil. Free Men vs. Socialist Wannabe Slaves' (cited in Serrano 1997).

© The Author(s) 2018

E. Bergmann, *Conspiracy & Populism*, https://doi.org/10.1007/978-3-319-90359-0_4

McVeigh repeatedly quoted and referred to white supremacist literature. He belonged to an anti-government survivalist militia movement, which, after the fall of communism shifted from warning of Soviet-conspiracies to ones aimed against the US federal government. They, for example insisted that US President Bill Clinton's campaign for gun control was a 'prelude to tyranny' (Russakof and Kovaleski 1995).

In letters to his sister, Jennifer, he seemed convinced that the government was plotting a dictatorial New World Order, and had already waged war against his people, his survivalist movement, insisting that he himself was merely a soldier responding to an attack and defending his country from the government oppressors (ibid.).

Timothy McVeigh was a frequent listener of the aforementioned conspiracy theorist, Milton William Cooper, an Oklahoma based radio show host who entangled UFO-ism with anti-government CTs. McVeigh was also plugged into the same network of Christian patriot movements as the so-called Hutaree, a Michigan based militia (Guarino 2010). Members of the paramilitary group believed that the federal government and various law enforcement agencies were all tangled up in a New World Order conspiracy, which the Hutaree pledged to stop (see Barkun 2013). In preparation for an end-of-time-battle with authorities, the Hutaree declared themselves 'Christian warriors.' Referring to the coming of an Antichrist they wrote: 'The Hutaree will one day see its enemy and meet him on the battlefield if so God wills it' (Schaeffer 2011).

The Oklahoma City bombing was just one of many violent acts conducted in the name of a good fight against evil domestic authorities. Often, such acts were carried out by lone wolf attackers like McVeigh. In April 2009, a 22-year-old man from Pittsburgh, Richard Poplawski, for example, opened fire with his semi-automatic assault rifle and killed three policemen. Poplawski feared that US authorities were out to get him and his gun owning friends. Online he had posted his suspicion that 'the federal government, mainstream media, and banking system in these United States are strongly under the influence of—if not completely controlled by—Zionist interest' (cited in Roddy 2009).

Timothy McVeigh was sentenced to death for the Oklahoma City bombing. He was executed in 2001. In 2012, several members of the Hutaree were arrested and prosecuted for planned violent attacks against government agents.

Surely, these sorts of domestic terrorists are out on the furthest fringes of far-right extremism and their actions resonate in no way with non-violent right-wing populists. Their extremism is much rather comparable with violent radical-left terror groups in Europe in the 1970s, and contemporary Islamist terrorists.

However, in recent years, Western societies have seen rising support for a variety of nationalist populist political parties (Bergmann 2017). And although most of them were much milder than these violent actors, they still tended to tap into similar political and philosophical sources—perhaps correspondingly to how the violent left tapped into socialist literature and Islamist terrorists based their horrific deeds on even mainstream religious texts.

This has led to the emergence of new political dividing lines. Political conflicts were no longer primarily flanked by the traditional left and right in an economic sense, but were increasingly polarized by conservative nationalists and internationalist liberals.

In this chapter, I attempt to frame contemporary right-wing nationalist populism. I explore its roots and map both the birth and development of populist movements in the post-war era in Europe.

Populism

When Richard Hofstadter (1964) published his famous book on CTs, *The Paranoid Style in American Politics*, the term populism—or what constituted being a populist—had not yet gained the same connotations it later contained in contemporary political studies. Still, present day populism can at least partially be fitted into his framework. As Noam Gidron and Bart Bonikowski (2013) point out, Hofstader's analysis of the paranoid style in American politics, 'characterized by heated exaggeration, suspiciousness and apocalyptic conspiratorial worldview' can also shed light on the 'properties of populist politics as a discursive style.' In a somewhat similar vein, Margaret Canovan (1981) saw populism as 'the shadow of democracy.'

In Hofstadter's view, populism was merely one of many other conspiratorial fantasies emanating from the political far-right. He saw the radical-right as standing psychologically outside the frame of normal democratic politics (cited in Mudde 2016). Thus, similar to CTs, populism has, in this regard, often been explained as a sort of *pathology* in post-war western societies, some sort of delusion and deviation from *normal* politics.

This view, however, does not always hold up in empirical testing. As will become evident in the following discussion, the spread of populism in contemporary Europe has proved to be much broader and reached further into the mainstream than can simply be dismissed or marginalised as paranoid and delusional. Similar to criticism against Hofstadter's views on CTs discussed in previous chapters, populism as such, is neither necessarily always pathological. In fact, just like is the case with CTs, populism can in certain situations be seen as a sensible world-view of the deprived and powerless, who are faced with a powerful capitalist order aligned against them. In that regard, it can be viewed as a legitimate strategy in the campaign for winning back lost authority from an overtly powerful elite. Thus, populism can be a useful tool in delegitimizing established authority and power relations.

Post-war Europe saw the rise of right-wing populist politics already in the 1970s, growing into ever stronger waves of populist nationalism in the 1990s and early 2000s. In 2014, right-wing populist parties won a record number of votes in the European Parliament elections. Populism rose even further in 2016, with the Brexit vote in the UK and election of Donald Trump to the White House in the USA. Recent years have seen the integration of populism into the mainstream in many countries, to the extent that it has become increasingly difficult to disentangle the two.

Populists can be either right or left wing. The fundamental difference between the two is, though, that while the right is preoccupied with the interests of the ordinary public, the left is particularly concerned with the socially underprivileged. Both, however, unite in criticism of the political elite, for example in the EU. Although right-wing nationalist populist movements have been established as a significant part of European politics since the 1970s, their reach has altered over time and across the continent. Usually they found greatest support amongst the rural less educated working class or unemployed males of the youngest and oldest age groups (Hainsworth 2008).

While usually avoiding referring openly to Mussolini's fascism or Hitler's Nazism, many of these movements still tapped into similar mixtures of nationalism, anti-capitalism and an emphasis on voluntary actions against elites. After the devastations of the Second World War, post-war fascists have tended to camouflage their origins, dressing their politics differently, as will be discussed later in this chapter. In his landmark book, *Anatomy of Fascism*, Robert Paxton (2004) warned that this has turned into an alibi for onlookers, that fascism, thus, was often overlooked in contemporary societies, most importantly in Western Europe, where he claimed fascists had always found the most fertile ground.

In an attempt to stem the electoral tide towards populist parties, many mainstream parties reverted to adopting some of their rhetoric, thus shifting the general political discourse in the populist direction and widening what was considered acceptable in public debate, as, for example, has occurred in Austria, Denmark and in the Netherlands (Grabow and Harleb 2013). Interestingly, though, there was not necessarily a correlation between actual social developments and their level of support. For example, both the True Finns and the Dutch Freedom Party grew stronger while immigration levels were falling in Finland and the Netherlands.

Definitions of populism have been quite fleeting in social science. Populist movements are of various kinds and usually tap into heritage and specific characteristics of their own nation rather than basing their politics on universal values. Still, they have many qualities in common as will be explored here. They all attempt to mobilize the masses and appeal to *the people* rather than *the elite*. Here, I focus on right-wing nationalist populism.

Before attempting to frame conspiratorial right-wing nationalist populism later in this chapter, I first turn to discussing a few underlying or related elements, such as nationalism and fascism and delve into mapping the recent rise of conspiratorialist populist parties in Europe.

Nationalism

Understanding nationalism can be a daunting task. The underlying concept of *nation* is even more challenging, perhaps one of the most nuanced in social sciences. Scholars have struggled in defining what constitutes a nation. In the late eighteenth century, German philosopher Johann Gottfried von Herder (1784) wrote that nations were almost natural phenomenon. He claimed that strong links existed between nature and nation; that traditions and habits in society emerge over a long period of time in relationship between nature and the nation. Furthermore, he said, the cultural essences of nations were kept in their languages, that it was, thus, languages that really set nations apart.

French intellectual, Ernest Renan (1882), disputed Herder's naturalist approach and claimed that nations were rather culturally constructed. In his view, a nation was similar to a soul, a spiritual principle, some sort of a moral conscience. Providing perhaps the only fully comprehensive definition to date, he said that distinguishable groups of people were a nation, simply if they consider themselves to be one: 'a nation is a daily plebiscite' he claimed. This, however, is far too general to be useful, even tautologically. In addition to Renan's definition, identities and qualities can be listed, which nations most often share to some extent. Amongst these can, for example, be a separate land, shared history, common language, ethnic origin, religion and other cultural elements. One problem with these sorts of criteria listing definitions is, though, that exceptions can always be found.

However, in this regard, nations are perhaps not natural, or only cultural, but also historically constructed. Nation rise; they can die out and new ones can emerge. Most often, nations share a common understanding of their history, and unify in a myth, which continues to be reproduced.

Nations can be constructed in various ways. German philosopher, Friedrich Meinecke (1908), developed the concepts of *Kulturnaton* and *Staatsnation* to distinguish between the different sorts of nationalism in Germany and France. On the one side, there were nations like the Germans who build their nationhood on a common cultural heritage. On the other were nations like France, which more often were constructed by a common political history and based on a constitution. This could be simplified by saying that in Germany, the nation had created the state, while in France, the state had created the nation.

Contemporary scholars such as Ernest Gellner (1983) and Anthony Smith (2002), view nations as social creations and thus contrast Herder's naturalist view. Still, however, Smith maintained that nations were much more firmly rooted than Renan claimed. According to Smith, nations—or ethnises more broadly—are 'named units of population with common ancestry myths and historical memories, elements of shared culture, some link with a historic territory and some measure of solidarity, at least among their elites' (Smith 2002). In his view, nations are logical and modern depictions of a deeply rooted common history and culture.

Gellner (1983) furthermore claimed that nations were created in social relations of people of a similar culture. Nationalism, he claimed, was 'primarily a principle which held that the political and national unit should be congruent.'

Eric Hobsbawn (1990) built on Gellner and claimed that nations were indeed creations of nationalism; without nationalism there were no nations. Similar to Renan, he considered 'any sufficiently large body of people whose members regard themselves as members of a "nation"' to be such. He emphasized that even though nations were created from above, it was necessary to study nationalism from the view below, that is, 'in terms of the assumptions, hopes, needs, longing and interests of ordinary people', who were the objects of the nationalistic message.

For the purpose of this book, irrespective of whether Renan's, Smith's, Gellner's or Hobsbawn's approaches are applied, nations can be seen as products of a common social understanding of those who belong to the national group. They are also most often a social and cultural creation of distinguishable group of people who unite around a common understanding of their shared history. It is this social creation that contemporary nationalist populists in Western societies tap into when constructing their discourse and framing their political message.

Nationalism parts from polarizing ideologies such as liberalism, anarchism, feminism, socialism and conservatism by its nature of encompassing the entire native population—this is a catch-all political approach. Still, nationalism has many faces and its factions can be compartmentalized by many different categories. Growing out of the

Enlightenment and Romanticism, nationalism, initially, coincided with demands for democracy in the eighteenth century. In its most elementary form, it was the demand that nations had an inherent right to establish sovereign states, governed by the people. Nationalism was, thus, a fundamental component of the struggle for democracy against absolutist monarchs in Europe, for example, leading up to the French Revolution. In that spirit, heroic endeavours of the French national army during the Prussian invasion of 1792 were, for example, praised in their national freedom song *Marseillaise*. After the revolutions of 1848, nationalists saw democracy as part of the struggle for national independence.

Nationalism spread rapidly through Europe and found its way into many of the European colonies. In this regard, nationalism was the struggle against oppression; this was, for example, instrumental in Palestine, Bosnia-Herzegovina, Lithuania, Cuba, Iraq and China. Nationalism also fuelled many separatist movements, for example, in Catalonia and the Basque region in Spain, Quebec in Canada and the Scottish movement in the UK.

In literature on political history in Europe, it is commonly accepted that the Westphalia peace agreement, signed in 1648, ending the 30 Years' War, gave birth to the still prevailing international system of independent nation-states. For the major part of human history, people had, however, lived in other political entities. Nationalism has proved to be a resilient ideology and the nation-state, as a political entity, emerged as the underlying source for legitimacy of the global order and the principle actor in international relations (Malesevic 2013). No other political order has emerged as a real alternative to the system of nation-states, which also has framed political identities in each of them. Identifying one's uniqueness is thus built into the very nature of nation-states, finding justification for its very existence by emphasizing what sets it apart from other nation-states (ibid.).

As will become clear in the coming discussion, and in following chapters, precisely this notion has provided one of the main ingredients in the winning formula of contemporary conspiratorial nationalist populist parties in Europe.

Fascism

Fascism emerges when political nationalism leads to authoritarianism, economic isolation and political extremism, based on viewing one's own nationality as above others. This sort of militant internal political nationalism can be traced to the writings of Italian intellectual Guiseppe Mazzini in the mid-nineteenth century (see Recchia and Urbinati 2010). Mazzini claimed that highest level of freedom was not of individuals but collective freedom of the nation: to reach higher freedom, he wrote, the individual surrenders his freedom over to the state. Since then, political nationalism travelled different routes, most notoriously emerging into fascism in Italy in the 1920s, and Nazi Germany in the 1930s, causing much of the pain Europe suffered in the twentieth century.

Born in Italy, the word fascism derives from *fascio*, literally a bundle of rods. Initially these were united bands of militarist nationalists declaring war on socialism. The fascist rhetorical platform rested not on a coherent political philosophy. Rather, they rejected compromise and harboured contempt for established society and the intellectual elite. While emphasizing their own leaders' mystical relationship with the ordinary public, most of these movements were chauvinistic, anti-capitalist and advocated voluntary violent actions against both socialist and bourgeois enemies (Paxton 2004). Their anti-capitalist rhetoric was, however, always very selective. Fascist regimes in government never did much to denounce capitalists, rather they dissolved labour unions and banned strikes. Similarly, they criticized the bourgeoisie for lack of loyalty to the nation rather than for exploiting the working class.

Internationalization and Migration

Nationalism, developing into fascism in the interwar years, had left the European continent in ruin in two devastating world wars. A new system of institutionalized international cooperation based on international law was to replace the fallen model of insulated sovereign nation states. An era of unprecedented level of internationalisation emerged. The Organization for Economic Cooperation in Europe (OEEC) was to manage generous US aid, named after Secretary of State, George Marshall. The Gold Standard, linking many of the most important world currencies, was temporarily resurrected, though on a quite different foundation, by the Bretton Woods agreement, also establishing the World Bank, and the International Monetary Fund.

The United Nations was established in 1949, giving its Security Council power to issue resolutions considered equal to international law. The North Atlantic Treaty Organization (NATO) was to bind security interests of European and American allies together through a firm collective military commitment on defence. Perhaps most importantly, to constrain rampant intra nationalism in Europe, the European economic integration process was initiated, developing into the supranational European Union (EU) of today, precisely in order to intertwine interests across borders so tightly that any military invasion would only hurt one's own interests.

Then, most of the European countries on the Western side of the Iron Curtain welcomed large number of foreign workers, to help resurrect the economy, and even quite physically, rebuild the continent out of the ruins. In the 1960s, immigrants were flocking to Europe from places like Turkey, India, Pakistan, North Africa, Sub-Saharan Africa and the Caribbean. Many came from far away colonies, bringing with them a new cultural flavour to the continent. Collectively, this was a liberal internationalist and, indeed, multicultural response to the devastations of war caused by nationalism (see Eicherngreen 2007).

Precisely this new internationalised architecture and increased migration soon became the target of many nationalist and right-wing populist conspiracy theorists, as here will be explored.

Cultural Racism

Despite this multicultural and internationally integrationist response to the devastations of the two world wars, nationalism was still always under the surface in the post-war years, though perhaps mostly dormant at first. Here, three waves of growth in the extreme-right since the Second World War can be identified (Bergmann 2017). Each wave rose in the wake of crisis, or major social change, and each grew stronger than the one before. All are identifiable by their own qualities and characteristics. First, prominent post-world-war movements, tapping into nationalist thought, rose in opposition to multiculturalism in the wake of the OPEC crisis in the 1970s; the second was brewing in the 1990s after the end of the Cold War and the third, in the wake of the international financial crisis in 2008. While still striving to avoid the risk of oversimplifying, analysing these waves can be helpful when studying nationalistic populist movements.

What sets these newer waves apart from earlier fascist movements is that contemporary nationalist populists do not denounce democracy. Secondly, and equally important, is that *biological* racism was replaced with *cultural* racism. In this transformation, arguments based on a racial hierarchy were replaced with an ethno-pluralist doctrine of 'equal but separate' (Rydgren 2005). Though humans were now considered biologically equal, culture still separated nations from each other. Nations were seen to form closed communities bounded by a common cultural identity. Claims for superiority by Europeans and the Western world came to rely on history rather than biology; often on an implicit but firmly underlying premise that Europeans were culturally superior (Wren 2001).

Similar to biological racism, cultural racism constructs closed and bounded cultural groups and 'conveniently legitimates the exclusion of "others" on the basis that they are culturally different' (Wren 2001). French new-right think tank, *Nouvell-Droite*, developed this doctrine based on a philosophical claim that nations had a right to cultural differences (McCulloch 2006).

Anders Jupskås (2015) furthermore claims that aggressive racist nationalism was replaced by a defensive nationalism promoting a mono-cultural society within the borders of the nation state. The new racist discourse thus relies on differentiating between *us* who belong to the cultural entity and *others* that are not part of the nationhood and, thus, don't belong. Within this discourse, the nation state creation in Europe is seen as a natural construction around cultural entities naturally developing. This proved to be a widely successful political framing and cultural racism has found a foothold in Europe since the 1970s, that is, in opposing cultural infiltration of *others* who don't belong to *our* cultural entity.

The new right surely tapped into nationalism of earlier periods but applied it in a non-violent way of normality, in what Michael Billing (1995) referred to as 'banal nationalism,' the everyday display of the nation in the public domain through a plethora of both explicit and subtle references. Referring to Renan, discussed earlier, this is the constant reproduction of the nation as a cohesive entity, which, as a result begs protection. The counter effect is the exclusion of *others*, such as immigrants, which perhaps was the very foundation of contemporary nationalist populist politics. Many of these parties have tended to apply abundant CTs aimed at explaining imminent external threats against the nation, while also identifying internal traitors of the nation.

Oil Crisis—First Wave

The first wave of right-wing nationalist populism in post-war Europe rose in the wake of the OPEC oil crisis hitting western Europe hard in the early 1970s and leading, for example, to a spike in unemployment. The first party to ride the wave was the French *Front National*,[1] founded and led by the colourful demagogue Jean Marie Le Penn. The party was directly constructed in opposition to post-war multiculturalism and immigration, mostly from Muslim countries.

Meanwhile, a different sort of right-wing populism was brewing in Denmark and Norway. Protesting against rising tax levels, the Danish and Norwegian Progress Parties (*Fremskridtspartiet, Fremskrittspartiet*) (FrP) promoted anarcho-liberalism and campaigned against an increased economic and bureaucratic burden on the ordinary man. They argued against wide scale social services, immigration and cosy consensus politics in these corporatist social-democratic welfare states. This was not the regular right-wing neo-liberal rhetoric, but rather a new populist version, where charismatic leaders positioned themselves alongside the blue collar public and against the political elite.

These movements offered an alternative voice to the mainstream in politics, tapping into fears of the ordinary public.

Skinheads emerged on the streets of many European capitals in the 1980s. Disgruntled youths were violently marching against immigrants, for example, in Britain, Germany, Italy and through Scandinavia. Revelling in fascist symbols, such as Nazi tattoos, wearing swastikas and playing loud white pride rock music, these demagogues were positioned on the fringes of society. Only later did nationalist populists disguise their neo-fascist nature with a more mainstream façade.

Collapse of Communism—Second Wave

Some of the populist parties finding success in the second and third wave were established before, sometimes initially as mainstream parties, only later turning populist. These include, for example, the Peoples Party of Switzerland (*Schweizerische Volkspartei*) and the Freedom Party of Austria (*Freiheitliche Partei Österreichs*—FPÖ), rising to power during the second wave in the 1990s. After retuning the party to a populist direction, by tapping into the fears and emotions of the ordinary public, while avoiding the more intellectual debate, the charismatic leader Jörg Haider moulded the FPÖ to become perhaps the most influential party in the country, entering the government in 2000. With a wink of approval to Nazi veterans, he told the people 'I say what you think' (cited in Grabow and Hartleb 2013). This, he was, however, only able to do with active support from the country's largest tabloid, the *Kronen Zeitung*. The tabloid joined in on the defiance against the elite, for example, turning against the established serious media elite. This was to become the recipe for populist parties' success throughout Europe: charismatic leaders backed by the tabloid media, relating to the ordinary public's fears of the foreign rather than participating in the intellectual political debate.

On that same type of platform, the Flemish block (*Vlaams Belang*) rose in Belgium as well as the Swiss Peoples Party, coming into government in 2004.

Similar trends were occurring in Italy where the neo-fascist Italian Allenza Nazionale had joined Silvio Berlusconi's first government a decade earlier, in 1994, and Umberto Bossi's Northern League (*Lega Nord*) was rising. The hooligan British National Party (BNP) was also building support in this period. In the Netherlands, Pim Fortuyn's List (*Ljist Pim Fortuyn*) claimed to be protecting Dutch liberalism against authoritarian Islamism. Geert Wilders' Freedom Party (*Partij voor de Vrijheid*), established after Fortuyn's murder in Amsterdam did, indeed, honour that liberalist heritage, while adding to the mix more general anti-Muslim rhetoric. Perhaps, most spectacularly, in riding the second wave of right-wing populism, Jean Marie Le Pen was, in 2002, able to manoeuvre his way into the second round of the French presidential election. After pushing Socialist candidate, Lionel Jospin, out, he stood against the right of centre President, Jacques Chirac, forcing the left to vote for its arch-rival in order to keep Front National out of the presidents' palace in Paris.

Conspiracy theories around immigrants ruining European culture served to reaffirm national identity, which became one of the main mobilizing factors in this period. The second wave, though, also rose partly in response to the anticipated integration with post-communist Eastern Europe—most of the newly free countries were expected to be joining the EU in the fullness of time.

This was also a time of rising nationalism throughout Eastern Europe in the wake of the collapsed communist model. Most notorious was ethnic cleansing in the Balkans. Populist nationalists rose in Russia and throughout the former eastern bloc. The Slovak National Party (*Slovenská Národná Strana*) was already established in 1990; in Poland, the Kaczynski brothers rose to power with their party Law and Justice (*Prawo I Sprawiedliwość*) and Lithuania similarly saw the rise of their version named Order and Justice (*Tvarka ir Teisingumas*). In a more militant style, the Jobbik-movement was gaining strength in Hungary, toying with full-blown neo-Nazism.

In Scandinavia, nationalist populism was also being remodelled during the second wave. On the ruins of Mogens Glistrup's Progressive Party, his former protégé, Pia Kjærsgaard, established the Danish

Peoples Party (*Dansk Folkeparti*—DF) in 1993. By carefully crafting her message to become more socially acceptable, the DF was fast moving into the mainstream, toning down the anti-tax rhetoric but still maintaining hard-core anti-immigrant policies. The DF campaigned against a multi-ethnic Denmark and an ongoing conspiracy of a foreign 'infiltration' into Danish society. Its 2002 manifesto, for example, stated that Denmark should belong to the Danes (Dansk Folkeparti 2002).

In Norway, Carl I. Hagen was steering his Progress Party towards the centre, to become perhaps the softest version of populist right-wing parties in Europe. The nature of the nationalism introduced in the second wave was different to that of the previous agrarian populism, or the anti-tax neo-liberal populism in the early 1970s. Rather than referring primarily to the social-economic situation of the *ordinary* people, the emphasis moved over to a socio-cultural notion of *our* people (Jupskas 2015).

When the Social Democrats in Europe, during the 1990s, after the collapse of the communist bloc, went looking for new voters and seeking more lucrative alliances in the centre, in what was branded the new economy—even in some places toying with neoliberal economic policies—the once strong links between the Social Democrats and the working class was rapidly evaporating. Becoming increasingly occupied with newer and more sophisticated political tasks, such as gender equality, administrative practices, democratic innovations, higher education and environmental protection, the Social Democratic parties were by the late twentieth century, losing support of the blue collar working class throughout Europe. Many of the traditional working-class voters on the left felt politically alienated, which allowed nationalistic populists to exploit the increased polarisation in society by filling the vacuum.

International Financial Crisis—Third Wave

In the wake of the international financial crisis in 2008, support for populist parties surged again in Europe, marking the rise of the third wave of post-war right-wing nationalism. As Cas Mudde (2004) introduced a few years earlier, this can be referred to as a populist *zeitgeist*, when populist discourse was moved from the fringes and into the mainstream—even adopted by government parties in some instances. The crisis shook the foundations of Western capitalism, bringing economic uncertainty, severe public austerity and increased hardship for the ordinary public, which largely felt victimized by both business and political elites. In this climate of fear and anger, nationalist populists found fertile ground for their conspiratorialist message criticizing the elites and campaigning against immigration and European integration, as well as, perhaps even more generally, the entire capitalist order, which they claimed was biased against the ordinary public.

Once again, after fine tuning their rhetoric in a more mainstream direction and away from open xenophobia, populist parties were finding much greater public support than before. In the UK, the more modest populist version, the UK Independence Party (UKIP), was replacing the openly racist BNP. In France, Front National found renewed support under the leadership of the more composed looking Marine Le Pen, who had replaced her more aggressive father, Jean-Marie Le Pen. In 2017, she swept through the political scene, easily graduating to the second round in the French presidential election and snatching up a staggering more than a third of the vote.

In Norway, Siv Jensen had in 2006, replaced the long-standing leader of the Progressive Party, Carl I. Hagen, eventually in 2013, landing the party in government as a coalition partner with the conservatives. In the 2017 parliamentary election, the party won more than 15% of the vote.

In Denmark, Pia Kjærsgaard had successfully moved the Danish Peoples Party from the fringes to be considered almost mainstream. She had done this by changing the discourse in the country, rather than modifying her message. In 2015, the DF bagged 21% of the vote.

In this period, more militant and openly racist parties were also gaining support in many other European countries. In Hungary, the Jobbik movement was still going strong, making populist premier Viktor Orbán, leader of the Fidesz party, almost look mainstream. Later, when Fidez had firmly occupied the nationalist right in Hungary, Jobbik moved closer to centre. In Bulgaria, the Attack Party (*Ataka*) was growing and in Greece, Golden Dawn was openly neo-Nazi. In Norway, notorious terrorist Anders Behring Breivik, responsible for the Utøya massacre in 2011—as was discussed at the beginning of this book—had left the Progressive Party, which he believed was too soft on immigration. He plugged into a loose knit underground network of militants, mostly communicating their racist message online below the surface.

Contrary to Denmark and Norway, where populist parties had been part of the political flora since the 1970s, such parties only saw rising support in the rest of the Nordic countries during the third wave. The Sweden Democrats (*Sverigedemokraterna*—SD) won their first seats in parliament in 2010, surging from 5 to 13% in 2014. Though its young leaders still had ties to Sweden's neo-Nazi past, and even while bringing forward a more chauvinistic nationalistic message than populists in neighbouring countries, the new version of this movement was able to transform itself enough to emerge as viable option to many disgruntled voters (Klein 2013). The True Finns (*Perussuomalaiset*), also found success during the third wave.

One of the greatest success of populist parties in the third wave came in the European Parliament elections of 2014. Most spectacularly, in three Western European countries, Denmark, France and the UK, populists surged to the very front. More militant fascist versions also saw significant gains, including the neo-fascist Golden Dawn, Jobbik in Hungary and Attack in Bulgaria. Euroscepticism was also finding its way to Germany with the rise of Alternative for Germany (*Alternative für Deutschland*), which secured significant support in the 2017 parliamentary election. Such sentiments were spreading in many of the more traditionally pro-EU countries.

As mentioned, these populist parties were a diffuse bunch with a variety of different approaches and often were solely focused on specific national situations in their home country. In 2015, the left-wing populist party, SYRIZA, found great electoral success in Greece on the canopy of the Euro crisis, in which it was able to exploit the many anti-EU CTs surging at the time. On similar grounds, Potemos rose in Spain. In Italy, the Five-star movement, founded by comedian Peppe Grillo, was also rising to new heights. In the 2018 parliamentary election, the party won almost a third of the votes, and the rebranded neo-racist Northern

League—now only named *Lega*—finished first within the coalition of right wing parties. This was the first time a populist party rose to the top in a founding member state of the EU.

Another kind of populism was sweeping through North America when flamboyant business tycoon, Donald Trump, was, against all odds, sworn into office as President of the United States in 2017, which is discussed further in the following chapter.

The move of the US Republican party towards right-wing populism, for example, was underlined when both former UKIP leader, Nigel Farage and Marion Maréchal-Le Pen, of the French Front National, were invited to address a high-level conservative and Republican gathering near Washington, DC in 2018, where both US President, Donald Trump, and Vice President, Mike Pence, were also amongst the speakers (Chrisafis 2018).

Integration into the Mainstream

Conventional wisdom constructed by many scholars said that populist political movements would not last, that they had the inbuilt difficulty of persistence. Many argued that they were bound to be only short-lived demagogues' protest movements flaring up briefly in wake of a crisis, before dying out (Canovan 2005), especially quickly after landing in government. The resilience of, for example, Front National in France, The Freedom Party in Austria, Progress Party of Norway and The Danish People's Party has, however, proven those predictions to be wrong. Rather, much of their conspiratorial message has prevailed over many decades. In many cases, they have been able to find legitimacy and sway the general national discourse in their own direction.

In fact, populist politics were fast being integrated much tighter into the mainstream. In Austria, for example, far-right populism was becoming firmly established as a prevalent element. Not only did the fully populist FPÖ re-enter government after winning more than a quarter of the vote in 2017, but the previously mainstream People's Party adopted much of the FPÖs hard-line stance on migration. The leading party in the collation of the two, the mainstream People's Party, had indeed almost fully adopted and internalised a rhetorical frame that previously was reserved only for describing a populist discourse (Opratko 2017).

Right-wing nationalist populism is well established in European politics, as has been illustrated here. In fact, recent years have seen an increased merging of populism into mainstream politics, to the extent that disentangling the two proves to be increasingly difficult. Contemporary Europe-wide opinion polls have, for example, shown that two thirds of the population think that their country has reached its limit in accepting migrants, and a staggering 85% agree with the following statement: 'Nowadays there is too much tolerance' (Mudde 2016). Anti-immigrant and authoritarian sentiments are, thus, not isolated on the fringes of society; they are no longer removed from the ordinary population. These are not views kept only within the minority ranks of the conspiratorial radical-right.

Erosion of Democratic Norms

The Western system of states, built after the Second World War—after the devastations of fascism and Naziism—was based on the values of liberal democracies. These broadly shared values included, for example: the rule of law, firm division of power, free trade across borders, systemic state cooperation, respect for human rights, wide reaching civil rights, unbiased and professional administration, and a free and independent media. These were some of the basic rules of Western democracies, respected across the political spectrum, from left to right. Politics, thus, did not challenge this commonly accepted frame, rather political adversaries campaigned for their policies firmly within these parameters. In other words, these were the outer limits of partisan pursuits.

One of the defining features of the populist political actors, discussed here, is found in their disrespect for this shared framework of Western liberal democracies. Many of them have, indeed, based their claim to power precisely on their willingness to undermine core norms of liberal democracy. It is exactly in their willingness to dispose of these shared democratic values where populists most clearly depart from mainstream parties and break away from the status quo. In fact, much of their appeal comes from challenging the established post WWII system—in fighting against what they brand as being the establishment.

In voicing their willingness to dismiss these formerly universal democratic values, the populists often accuse the establishment of betraying the people, and, as is discussed throughout this book, quite often communicate their anger by way of CTs.

In the process, discredited authoritarian leaders of the past, such as Mussolini and Stalin, are again being glorified, and notorious policies that for a long time were collectively dismissed—such as of religious and racial segregation—are rising to the surface again. Jörg Haider of Austria, for instance, dismissed much of the discussion around Austria's Nazi past, and the leader of the Italian *Lega*, Matteo Salvini, openly voiced his admiration of Mussolini (see Mounk 2018). In Russia, Putin has repeatedly moved to resurrect Stalin's reputation.

Another aspect of this change—when shared rules of political conduct are being contested—is found in an ongoing move away from merely seeing political opponents as adversaries who are all competing within a level playing field and according to shared rules. Instead, opponents are increasingly being turned into enemies. As Michael Ignatieff (2013), political theorist and former leader of the Liberal party of Canada, wrote. 'An adversary is someone you want to defeat. An enemy is someone you have to destroy.'

The process of normalization of populist politics, for example, occurs when mainstream parties follow suit in wake of the populists, and in their quest for winning back lost supporters, themselves start to abandon the once shared values of Western democracies. This, in turn, begins the process of eroding once shared democratic norms of the West.

Cas Mudde (2016) maintains that the populist radical-right constitutes a radicalization of mainstream views, that key aspects of populist radical-right conspiratorialism is now being shared by the mainstream. Still, although populism is increasingly being entangled into the mainstream, that does not absolve us from the responsibility of framing the phenomena.

Framing Nationalist Populism

Defining what constitutes populist politics and populist political movements can, though, be a difficult task. Not only can populism be understood as either an ideology or a rhetorical style, but also, these are often quite different groupings, holding a variety of positions, which can be changeable from country to country and, most often, constructed around respective national interests, which could, as well, be contradictory across borders. Often, they are even at odds with each other. UKIP in Britain, for example, refused to cooperate with the French National Front in the European Parliament, which they accused of being racist (Newman 2014).

Many of the populist movements held neo-liberal economic policies, while others were mostly concerned with protecting the welfare system from infiltration of foreign immigrants—for the benefit of the ethnic population. This was, for example, the case in Scandinavia, where, interestingly, populist movements in the 1970s had started out being neo-liberal. Modest versions of populist movements existed; some were primarily nationalist; they could be far-right or what can be called extreme far-right, sometimes even a militant version denouncing democracy. There were those of a more fascist nature, mostly found in Eastern Europe, but also in Greece and other Western European countries, including, for example, Sweden. Then there were also left-wing versions.

Margaret Canovan (1981) maintained that there existed many different traits of populism, each rooted in their own social and historical context. Populist politics is, thus, a broad church and populism, as such, does not fit into one particular ideology. It is not a well-squared set of rational policies. As was the case with nationalism discussed earlier, any populist movement, though, aimed to mobilize the masses; it was an appeal to the people rather than the elite. They were catch-all rather than class based.

The influential analyst of European right-wing populism, Cas Mudde (2007), describes radical-right-populism as a 'thin-centred ideology' separating society into two homogenous and antagonistic groups: 'the pure people' versus 'the corrupt elite,' emphasizing the 'general will' of the people. The people are, here, interpreted as a homogeneous moral entity (Mudde 2016). According to this approach, the main aim of politics should be realising the will *of* the people, rather than the elite being allowed to impose their will *on* the people. Here, the people are almost seen as sacred and being unassailable.

This is comparable to CTs: to a Manichean outlook of politics, casting politics as a binary struggle between the *people* and the undeserving self-serving *political class.* Or as Daniele Albertazzi and Duncan McDonnel (2007) put it, populists 'pit a virtuous and homogenous people against a set of elites and dangerous "others" who are depicted as depriving the sovereign people of their property and rights.' In Kirk Hawkins' (2003) analysis, politics is seen by the populists as a struggle between *good* and *evil.* Ideologically, right-wing nationalist populism is thus defined on the socio-cultural dimension, rather than on the socio-economic axis.

Herbert Kitschelt introduced what he called the 'winning formula' of right-wing populism, which combined neo-liberal politics with authoritarianism and a policy of anti-immigration (Kitschelt and McGann 1997). Alternatively, populism can also be seen as a style or technique of political mobilization and communication (Grabow and Hartleb 2013).

Andreas Schedler (1996) identified populism primarily with a broad array of anti-attitudes: anti-elite, anti-establishment, anti-modern, anti-urban, anti-industrial, anti-state, anti-foreign, anti-intellectual and anti-minority sentiments. Taken collectively, populists are perhaps most simply 'Nay-sayers' who resist change as Hans Georg Betz (2001) claimed. In effect, they strive to stop modernization and social change. What sets contemporary right-wing nationalist populists apart from earlier fascist and Nazist versions who favoured authoritarian leadership is that most of them now accept democracy and parliamentarianism. They are thus much rather anti-elite than anti-system.

Whichever viewpoint from the differing definitions we choose, some similarities can still be identified, which might help in framing the phenomena.

Common Qualities

In my own analysis (see Bergmann 2017), I identify ten common qualities which nationalist populists most often have in common. First of all, right-wing populists in Europe are nationalist. Within a nostalgic frame, they are prone to apply myths in order to bring people together within common and cohesive national boundaries. Secondly, and most obviously, they campaign against multiculturalism and strive to stem the flow of immigration. Thirdly, they are usually nativist and exclusionary. They divide between *us* who belong to society and *them* who should not belong to it. Who *they* are can be, for example, immigrants, asylum-seekers, ethnic or religious minorities, even the political elite. The *others* are discursively turned into enemies of *us*, threatening *our* identity and culture or exploiting and, thus, ruining the welfare state *we* have built. *Others* are here clearly distinguished from the ethnic natives, *us*. This often results in open xenophobia and racism. In Western Europe, this is most often aimed against Muslims, for example, in Austria, Denmark, France and the Netherlands, while in Eastern Europe, the targets are often Roma people or even Jews, as was the case in earlier times.

Fourthly, populist movements often revolve around a strong charismatic leader. Most often they relied on what they claim to be a special relationship between the leader and the ordinary public. Particularly, the leader is often seen to understand the burdens of the ordinary public, which, vitally, is being overlooked by the established political elite. The populist leader, on the other hand, usually claims to know how to solve their problems.

This brings forward the fifth shared characteristic. Populists are anti-intellectual and anti-elitist, even though their leaders themselves often tend to come from the same privileged background as the elite. They claim to be advocates of the nation and seek to speak in her name. In doing so, they differentiate between honest ordinary people and the corrupt elite and discursively turn them into two homogeneous and antagonistic groups. One of their main successes recently has, indeed, been in criticizing consensus politics of the corrupt political elite.

Sixth, the message for solving the ordinary public's most pressing problems tend to be simple: these are straightforward solutions to meet complex national interests. Often, they call for mobilizing answers, such as cleansing of foreign parasites. They tend to speak to emotions rather than to reason and avoiding more intellectual debate.

Seventh, populism is rather moralistic than practical. Populists often have no problem with contradictions, for example, simultaneously promoting economic liberalism and the lowering of taxes while promising increased welfare services and easy implementation of high cost policies.

Eigth, while often claiming to be economically liberal, populists are more usually protectionist of national production from international competition, especially in the field of agriculture. Often, they exploit a lack of confidence, for example, in the wake of crisis. They voice the dissatisfaction of those losing out to increased globalization and rapid social change.

Ninth, populist parties are usually authoritarian and social conservatives, they believe in a strictly ordered society and are rather defined on socio-cultural aspects than on the socio-economic scale. They are, thus, not necessary positioned on the classical economic right. They emphasize family values and law and order, often claiming that the system protects criminals rather than their victims amongst the ordinary public. Another aspect here is that they disproportionally bring attention to crimes conducted by alien forces, such as migrants.

Finally, populists in Europe are most often staunchly Eurosceptic. Some only talk about stemming further integration, while others strive to push back Europeanization and even abolish the European Union.

When tying these elements together, a picture emerges: Right-wing populists in Europe are nationalist, anti-immigrant, anti-elitist, anti-intellectual and Eurosceptic moralists who are economically protectionist, promoters of law and order and against multicultural development on the continent. They speak to emotions rather than reason; they are nativists who distinguish between *us* and *them* and rely on strong charismatic leaders who advocate simple solutions to complex issues burdening the ordinary individual.

Taken collectively, right-wing nationalist populists put forth a threefold claim in support of the people: First, they discursively create an external threat to the nation; second, they accuse the domestic *elite* of betraying the *people*, often of even siding with the *external* forces; third, they position themselves as the only true defenders of the pure people they vow to protect against these malignant outsiders, that is, against those that they themselves have discursively created.

These features might help in identifying the links in the literature between populism and CTs, which I turn to next.

Note

1. At the party congress in March 2018, the leader of the party, Marine Le Pen, proposed rebranding it and renaming it as *Rassemblement National*. In this book, however, I use the name *Front National* (FN) throughout.

References

Albertazzi, D., & McDonnell, D. (2007). *Twenty-first century populism: The spectre of Western European democracy*. Basingstoke: Palgrave Macmillan.

Barkun, M. (2013). *A Culture of Conspiracy: Apocalyptic Visions in Contemporary America*. Berkeley: University of California Press.

Bergmann, E. (2017). *Nordic nationalism and right-wing populist politics: Imperial relationships and national sentiments*. London: Palgrave Macmillan—Springer.

Betz, H.-G. (2001). Exclusionary populism in Austria. Italy and Switzerland. *International Journal, 53*(3), 393–420.

Billig, M. (1995). *Banal nationalism*. London: Sage.

Canovan, M. (1981). *Populism*. New York: Harcourt Brace Jovanovich.

Canovan, M. (2005). *The people*. Cambridge: Polity.

Chrisafis, A. (2018). Marion Maréchal-Le Pen to share stage with US conservatives. *The Guardian*. London.

Dansk Folkeparti. (2002, October). *Party programme of the Danish People's Party*. Retrieved from danskfolkeparti.dk.

Eicherngreen, B. (2007). *The European economy since 1945: Coordinated capitalism and beyond*. Princeton: Princeton University Press.

Gellner, E. (1983). *Nations and nationalism*. Ithaca: Cornell University Press.

Gidron, N., & Bonikowski, B. (2013). *Varieties of populism: Literature review and research agenda* (Working Paper Series). Weatherhead Center for International Affairs, Harvard University, no. 13-0004. Retrieved from papers.ssrn.com.

Grabow, K., & Hartleb, F. (2013). Mapping present-day right-wing populists. In Brabow & Hartleb (Eds.), *Exposing the demagogues: Right-wing and national populist parties in Europe*. Berlin: Konrad Adenauer Stiftung.

Guarino, M. (2010, 31 March). *Could the Hutaree militia have spawned a Timothy McVeigh?* Boston: The Christian Science Monitor.

Hainsworth, P. (2008). *The extreme right in Western Europe*. Abingdon-on-Thames: Routledge.

Hawkins, K. (2003). Populism in Venezuela: The rise of Chavismo. *Third World Quarterly, 24*(6), 1137–1160.

Hobsbawn, E. (1990). *Nations and Nationalism since 1780: Programme, Myth, Realitiy*. Cambridge: Cambridge University Press.

Hofstadter, R. (1964). *The paranoid style in American politics*. New York: Vintage Books.

Ignatieff, M. (2013, October 16). Enemies vs. Adversaries. *New York Times*. New York.

Jupskås, A. R. (2015). *The persistence of populism. The Norwegian Progress Party 1973–2009*. Faculty of Social Sciences, University of Oslo, no. 527.

Kitschelt, H., & McGann, A. J. (1997). *The radical right in Western Europe: A comparative analysis*. Ann Arbor: University of Michigan Press.

Klein, A. (2013). The end of solidarity? On the development of right-wing populist parties in Denmark and Sweden. In Grabow & Hartleb (Eds.), *Exposing the demagogues: Right-wing and national populist parties in Europe*. Berlin: Konrad Adenauer Stiftung.

Kovalski, S., & Russakof, D. (1995, 2 July). *An Ordinary Boy's Extraordinary Rage*. Washington: The Washington Post.

Malesevic, S. (2013). *Nation-states and nationalisms: Organization, ideology and solidarity*. Cambridge: Polity.

McCulloch, T. (2006). The Nouvelle Droite in the 1980s and 1990s: Ideology and entryism, the relationship with the Front National. *French Politics, 4*(2), 158–178.

Meeting between Swedish and Norwegian ministers scrapped following "no-go zone" claims. (2017, August 29). Oslo: The local.no.

Meinecke, F. (1908). *Cosmopolitanism and the national state*. Princeton: Princeton University Press.

Milne, R. (2017, August 30). Norway minister sparks war of words with Sweden over immigration. *The Financial Times*. London.

Mounk, Y. (2018). *The people vs. democracy: Why our freedom is in danger & how to save it*. Cambridge: Harvard University Press.

Mudde, C. (2004). The populist Zeitgeist. *Government and Opposition, 39*(4), 541–563.

Mudde, C. (2007). *Populist radical right parties in Europe.* Cambridge: Cambridge University Press.

Mudde, C. (2016). *On extremism and democracy in Europe.* Abingdon-on-Thames: Routledge.

Newman, C. (2014, May 29). A canny Nigel Farage is right to shun Marine Le Pen's advances. *The Telegraph.* London.

Opratko, B. (2017, October 23). Austria's right turn. *Jacobin Magazine.* New York. Retrieved from jacobinmag.com.

Paxton, R. (2004). *The anatomy of fascism.* London: Penguin Books.

Recchia, S., & Urbinati, N. (2010). *A cosmopolitanism of nations: Giuseppe Mazzini's writings on democracy, nation building and international relations.* Princeton: Princeton University Press.

Renan, E. (1882). *Qu'est-ce qu'une nation?* Paris: Sorbonne.

Roddy, D. (2009, 10 April). *An Accused Cop Killer Politics.* New York: Slate. com.

Rydgren, J. (2005). Is extreme right-wing populism contagious? Explaining the emergence of a new party family. *European Journal of Political Research, 44*(3), 413–437.

Schaeffer, F. (2011, June). *Sex, Mom, and God.* ReadHowYouWant.com.

Schedler, A. (1996). Anti-political-establishment parties. *Party Politics, 2*(3), 291–312.

Serrano, R. (1997, 9 December). *Witnesses Say McVeigh Didn't Refer to Nichols.* Los Angeles: LA Times.

Smith, A. D. (2002). *Nations and nationalism in global era.* Cambridge: Polity.

von Beyme, K. (1988). *Right-wing extremism in Western Europe.* London and New York: Routledge.

von Herder, J. G. (1784). *Ideen zur Philosophie der Geschiche der Menschheit.* CreateSpace Independent Publishing Platform (19 February 2013).

Wren, K. (2001). Cultural racism: Something rotten in the state of Denmark? *Social and Cultural Geography, 2*(2), 141–162.

5

Disrupting the Trust—Nature of Populist CTs

Unlike many other Brits, who midday on 16 June 2016 were preparing for watching the Euro 2016 football clash between England and Wales, a 52-year-old unemployed Scottish-born man living in Birstall in the UK had his mind elsewhere. Instead, Thomas Mair rushed to front of the Market Street library in his West Yorkshire town, pulled out a sawn-off rifle and knife and shot and stabbed a 41-year-old woman who in the early afternoon was heading for the library entrance.

Jo Cox was a Labour MP on her way to a constituency surgery. She died as result of multiple wounds and Mair was sentenced to life in prison without the possibility of pardoning. This was the first murder of a British parliamentarian since the Provisional Irish Republican Army (IRA) assassinated Conservative Ian Gow in 1990.

The horrendous killing of Joe Cox occurred just a week before the referendum on the exit of the UK from the European Union—Brexit— on 23 June 2006. Cox was a staunch believer in European integration and a firm supporter of both immigrants and a liberal multicultural British society. Similar to Norwegian terrorist, Anders Behring Breivik, discussed at the beginning of the book, her killer, on the other hand, had come to believe that left-wing liberals in politics and in the

© The Author(s) 2018
E. Bergmann, *Conspiracy & Populism*, https://doi.org/10.1007/978-3-319-90359-0_5

mainstream media were responsible for much of the world's evil and, indeed, for his own misfortune (Bennett 2016).

Mair was a racist, obsessed with notions of white people facing increasing aggression. He had utmost contempt for those he called white traitors of their own people. In his eyes, Cox was one of these left liberals responsible for ruining the Western world, one of 'the collaborators' of these external aggressors and a 'traitor to white people' (cited in Cobain et al. 2016).

Thomas Mair was plugged into many far-right groups, including the National Front and the notorious English Defence League, where he attended many gatherings. His house was filled with Nazi memorabilia and white supremacy literature. Noticeably, he had, for example, kept press cuttings about the case of Anders Breivik.

'My name is death to traitors, freedom for Britain.' This was the reply Mair gave when asked in the Westminster Magistrates Court to confirm his name (cited in Booth et al. 2016). He had a long history of mental health problems. During the case procedure, it became evident that he had been influenced by much of the rhetoric upheld by the nationalist right in the Brexit campaign. Witnesses before the court testified that during the attack, he had cried out 'this is for Britain,' 'keep Britain independent,' and 'Put Britain first' (cited in Cobain and Taylor 2016).

The judge on the case said there was no doubt that Mair had murdered Cox 'for the purpose of advancing a political, racial and ideological cause, namely that of violent white supremacism and exclusive nationalism most associated with Nazism and its modern forms' (BBC News 2016).

It stands to reason, of course, that the politicians and activists campaigning for Brexit in the UK at the time cannot be held directly responsible for this horrendous act of a madman. Still, however, it is equally impossible to completely escape from the fact that political messages are sometimes received in different ways than they are intended to be interpreted.

As was evident from discussions in the two preceding chapters, CTs and populism share many attributes—here mixed in a vicious cocktail by murderer Thomas Mair.

In this chapter, I explore common tropes of the two strands, and attempt to frame populist CTs and identify how they are applied in politics.

Common Tropes

Similar to tendencies of populists (Chapter 4), who make a distinction between the *innocent public* and *malignant elite*—countering *pure people* and *a corrupt elite*—conspiracy theorists (Chapter 3) also tend to utilize similar duality: clearly dividing between the *unknowing people,* and their *conspirators* who are in a position of power.

This is what Steven Van Hauwaert (2012) calls shared duality of both populism and CTs. Like populists, the conspiratorial world is similarly divided between 'good versus evil, right versus wrong, victims versus conspirators.' Potok and Terry (2015b) argue that the far-right increasingly identifies evil-doers in politics, who are seen to conspire against the ordinary public—for example, the global elites who are secretly conspiring to create a totalitarian New World Order.

Perhaps most obviously, thus, both populists and conspiracy theorists unite in a *Manichean* worldview, discursively creating an external threat to the inner group. Both strands offer the same binary scheme to understand events and state of affairs, based on a similar polarised world-view. Put another way, both strands share a joint archetypical storytelling narrative, in which a heroic underdog is fighting a powerful evil villain. One of the main identifying features of right-wing populism is, thus, found in its polarizing division between *the people* and *the elite.* As Michael Barkun (2013) has identified, this dualism has proved to be very powerful, indeed an 'ideal vehicle for apocalyptic anxieties.'

Despite many shared attributes, distinctions between the two strands can still be detected when it comes to kinds of dualism. While populists tend to oppose the corrupt elite with the pure people conspiracy theorists tend, rather, to counter conspirators with the unknowing people (Hauwaert 2012).

As was analysed in Chapter 4, another main feature of populism is offering simple solutions to complex problems. Similarly, the simplicity

of CTs—solving complex issues by pointing to a single grand plot—
is also one of the main appeals of CTs. Mark Fenster (1999) however
maintains that CTs depart from populist analysis, who both might offer
a simplistic vision of antagonism between the *people* and the *elites*, by
offering incredibly detailed analyses of complex power relations.

Although the two strands share many attributes, as here has been
illustrated—such as not much minding contradictions in their narrative—the relationship between populism and CTs is, however, often
ambiguous. Still, studies have shown that a belief in CTs correlates
highly with being susceptible to populist politics. Those who see the system as being stacked against them have been found far more likely to
both believe in CTs and support populist political parties (Oliver and
Rahn 2016). They are likely to have less trust in society and to be angry
at authorities. Furthermore, both strands share anti-elitism and mistrust
of experts. CTs and populism, thus, tend to complement each other.

Political Arena

In his celebrated book, *The Open Society and Its Enemies*, philosopher
Karl Popper (1945) famously said that totalitarianism was founded
on CTs. He discusses what he called the 'conspiracy theory of society,'
describing a world-view in which explanations of a social phenomenon were mainly focused on 'the discovery of the men or groups who
are interested in the occurrence of this phenomenon,' and 'who have
planned and conspired to bring it about.' Popper maintained that this
view arises from the 'mistaken theory that, whatever fallacies happens in
society—such as war, unemployment, poverty, shortages—is the result
of direct design by some powerful individuals and groups.'

Popper's analysis of a world-view which always assumes intention
behind political devolvement is still relevant as CTs have, in recent
years, increasingly moved onto the political arena. Like populism in
general, they also tend to spread most rapidly in the wake of a crisis.
Political CTs, thus, usually rise in the aftermath of some sort of societal
predicament. It is therefore not surprising that the interwar years proved

to provide a fertile ground for CTs to grow. The Nazi's were, for example, firmly anti-Masonic and saw implications of a secret New World Order seizing control after the German defeat in WWI. Indeed, 1936 was a year of nationalist CTs. At the time, both Mussolini in Italy and Hitler in Germany, for example, toyed with millennialism.

The Nazis saw Jewish conspiracies everywhere. They insisted, for example, that Jews were using their wealth against the interests of the German nation (Byford 2011). In Germany, the media was filled with anti-Jewish CTs. A fear had spread around the country of a Zionist New World Order plot. We know all too well what happened next.

Without comparing the present situation with the 1930s, we now see that CTs are again spreading across the political arena in the Western world. Recently, they have increasingly come to revolve around issues having more direct consequences on contemporary socio-political developments, such as European integration and globalization. Byford (2011) argues that CTs have, indeed, become a popular means of 'articulating an opposition to the forces of international capitalism, globalism' and the 'rise of a transnational political order.'

Actors within the global system, such as the Bilderberg group, are suspected of plotting against the people across borders. Elites in contemporary Western countries are seen to all be entangled in a 'global plutocracy of self-interested politicians, media leaders and capitalists' (Potok 2017). As was discussed in the previous chapter, this rhetoric was, for example, upheld during the Greek economic crisis, starting in 2008, where rumours were floating around of malignant intensions of, for example, the IMF and the EU apparatus.

Suspicions of international actors and institutions, however, have a long history. While Marxists mainly focused on global capitalist plots, Christian millenialists were often occupied with notions of an Antichrist. Some came to regard the League of Nations, established in 1920, as an institution awaiting an Antichrist coming to control life on earth (Barkun 2013). Ever since then, many have become wary of international institutions and global actors. As result, right-wing populists have tended to promote conspiratorial arguments against the post-war international order, which was discussed in the previous chapter.

Amongst common themes of CTs has been suspicions of global elites secretly establishing a totalitarian New World Order. In the US, many such CTs have been aimed against the North America Free Trade Agreement (NAFTA), insisting that elites in the USA, Canada and Mexico were covertly planning to merge the three countries into a single super-state (Potok and Terry 2015a).

Furthermore, anti-government patriot groups—like those Timothy Mc Veigh, for example, belonged to—are abundant in the US and scattered all over the country. Many of them believe that the US government is covertly conspiring to deprive US citizens of their civil liberties (Potok 2017).

Many separatist militias of this world also tended to base their politics on CTs. Byford (2011) for example found that CTs were the dominant paradigm in Slobodan Milosevic's regime in Serbia in the 1990s and, indeed, the main rhetoric used for interpreting the Yugoslav conflict. The same was true in Hugo Chavez's Venezuela, where CTs of foreign aggression were used to justify, not only the bad shape of the domestic economy, but also the suppression of political dissidents in the troubled country, who were accused of betraying their nation on behalf of the foreign aggressors.

Conspiracy theories are entangled into politics in many ways. Perhaps one of the most interesting conspiracy theorists in politics was Jacques Cheminade, a French far-left three-time presidential candidate and leader of the party Solidarity and Progress (*Solidarité et progress*), the French arm of the *LaRouche* movement. Cheminade, for example, insisted that HIV was created by the Soviets in laboratories as a weapon. In 1984, he accused French Socialist President, François Mitterrand, of not only being a 'Soviet agent' but also a servant of an international fascist movement established in the 1920s.

Cheminade (1996) began to view Britain as the source of much of the world's evil. He insisted that the neighbour north of the Channel was—with help from the domestic elite in Paris—setting out to destroy the French nation-state. In 1996, he wrote, for example, that 'the British-French "Entente Cordiale" is, today, the main threat to world history.' He went on to say that 'Napoleon, like Hitler, was first promoted by the British, as were the Jacobins before them, to destroy France, and to prevent a truly republican option.'

Cheminade (2000) claimed that all governments in France, since at least the 1980s, had 'continuously and persistently betrayed the sovereignty of their nation-state.' Because of that, he was, for example, suspicious of the death of Princess Diana in Paris in 1997 and wrote that officials of France's Socialist government had supervised her death on behalf of the British. He furthermore claimed that both John F. Kennedy and Martin Luther King were killed by the same people as those that had tried to murder French President, Charles de Gaulle, and 'for the same oligarchical reasons.'

Next, I turn to discuss specific far-right populist CTs.

Disrupting the Trust

Conspiracy theories can be tailored to any political view. And while populism is surely variously found on the political spectrum, the two unite as an especially powerful force within the field of the nationalist far-right. As has been established here, far-right populists who subscribe to anti-immigrant CTs have, in some instances, tended to turn to violence. Many have become convinced of their just cause of defending their society against an external threat that society is facing and against the domestic elite, which they believe has betrayed the public.

For many populists, CTs have also become the answer to explaining their own misfortune. As is evident from horrendous actions of some of the individuals discussed here, such as Norwegian terrorist Anders Behring Breivik, US terrorist Timothy McVeigh and Jo Cox's murderer in Britain, Thomas Mair, they tend to justify the violence as a defence against external evil.

Indeed, CTs remain the main ingredient of most extremist groups. Not only those on the far-right but also most others, for example, of many Islamist terrorists, such as Isis. In all cases, the scapegoats are always outsiders, never those who belong to the in-group in society. Instead they are always *The Other*, never *Us*. Populist CTs can, thus, come to erode trust in society.

In recent years, trust has been at an all-time low in western societies (*The Economist* 2016). Voters have increasingly turned against their mainstream politicians and towards those that claim to *tell-it-as-it-is*, to actors that *speak their mind* and *don't mince their words*—in other words, to political operators that are less cautious and less professional.

Studies have found that CTs in politics serve to discourage people from voting or participating in politics. More specifically, Karen Douglas (2017) found that 'people felt less inclined to vote because the CTs made them feel politically powerless.' Mark Potok and Don Terry (2015b) conclude that populist CTs are destructive to democracy, as they 'substitute ignorance and suspicion for knowledge and reason.'

Many scholars—such as Barkun (2013) and Byford (2011)—have established a direct link between extremism in practise and belief in CTs. Imhoff and Bruder (2014) furthermore found a positive liner relationship between right-wing authoritarianism and belief in CTs. Jamie Bartlett and Carl Miller (2010) document that in the context of extremism, acceptance of CTs often serves as what they term as 'radicalizing multiplier,' which suggest that supporters of populists are more prone than others to subscribe to CTs.

The extreme-right has indeed proved to be increasingly conspiratorial in their political discourse. Jamie Bartlett and David Miller (2010) of the British think tank, Demos, identify a three-way causal chain in their study. First, they claim that 'conspiracy theories create demonologies of "the other" or "the enemy"' that the group defines itself against. Second, they delegitimise voices of dissent and moderation by casting them as part of the conspiracy. Finally, they can encourage a group to turn to violence, acting as rhetorical devices to portray violence, both to the group itself and their wider supporters, as necessary to 'awaken the people from their acquiescent slumber.'

In a study by Jan-Wihelm van Prooijen et al. (2015), it was similarly established that CTs can be a catalyst for radicalization and extremism—that they fuel violence, for example, by encouraging unstable people to act against authorities who they perceive as conspiring against them. In this regard, CTs can be seen as posing a danger to society. Ergo, similarly to populists more broadly, CTs often serve to disrupt the trust between the people and their governments.

Populist Conspiratorialism

The most striking feature in the discourse of populist political parties has indeed often tended to be CTs. As was discussed in Chapter 3, Richard Hofstadter saw CTs as an expression of populist protest, a form of radical populist discourse. More specifically, Mark Fenster (1999) says they express the views of those that perceive a secret elite dominating and manipulating 'the entirety of economic, political and social relations.'

Classical CTs of far-right and neo-Nazi groups have, for example, revolved around ideas of a totalitarian New World Order being plotted against the Christian white community. The plotters are often seen to be, for example, a mixture of liberals, Marxists, homosexuals, feminists and others of similar kind who have taken control of both the government and the media. Another version is suspecting a band of Jews controlling world governments, the theory of a Zionist Occupied Government.

In their content analysis of literature, ideology and propaganda of more than fifty extremist groups, Bartlett and Miller (2010) found that most of them firmly apply CTs in their discourse. Interestingly, among most of these groups anti-Semitism was still a central theme. These findings were, for instance, supported in a study conducted by Mari-Liis Madisson (2016) into groups of the Estonian extreme-right. She concluded that CTs were indeed the dominant framework of their political discourse.

In the USA, the John Birch society and many other anti-government patriot movements staunchly believe that the government is secretly planning to impose martial law and confiscate all privately held guns in America (Potok and Terry 2015b). In many versions, this gun-grabbing suspicion is only a prelude to an imposition of a totalitarian world government.

The radical-right has also tapped into some of the more far-fetched classical CTs, such as New Ages theories, tales of UFOs, prophesies like that of Nostradamus and notions of an Illuminati-like New World Order. Juxtapositioning these with anti-government theories of the far-right has led to many sorts of innovative hybrid theories. These often inconspicuous constructions, were stirred up again, for example, in the wake of the 9/11 attacks, mainly within militarist radical-right subcultures (Barkun 2013).

Potok and Terry (2015a) identify ten main CTs, which they say are upheld by the far-right in the US. In addition to fears of Marxists seeking to unarm Americans to prepare for their occupation of the country, and tales of President Obama not being US-born, they also include suspicions of: a homosexual agenda ending civilization; military exercises being a prelude to the government instating martial law; Sharia law being implemented in parts of the USA, and of numerous secret Muslim training grounds being scattered around the USA waiting to occupy America. This last one is the subject of next chapter.

Before viewing in more detail four cases, or examples of populist CTs later in this chapter, I first turn to examining CTs promoted by the powerful, more generally.

Of the Powerful

It has long been established that CTs thrive on insecurity and fear—on a feeling of disempowerment. This is why Joe Uscinski and Joe Parent (2014) concluded that CTs are, mainly, for losers. Most of the literature on CTs has, henceforth, focused on the powerless. Interestingly, however, political CTs are also being upheld by the powerful elite, from the very power centres themselves. When studying CTs, it is thus important to separate between those in society that receive and subscribe to them and the political actors that produce and promote them for political gain.

Before delving into contemporary CTs of the powerful, we should, however, firmly recognize that the political elites have, of course, through history often engaged in all kinds of scare mongering. In and off itself, that is, of course, nothing new. Indeed, rumours, lies and rhetorical manipulations have been common tactics used by leaders throughout the centuries. To divide and conquer is a long-time favorited strategy of most dictators and, also, many democratic leaders.

Creating antagonism and spreading fear against external threats was, for instance, one of the tools Machiavelli (1550) promoted in his famous book, *The Prince*—which was written as kind of political strategy guideline for Renaissance Italy. Conspiracy theories have often been upheld by authoritarian regimes to crush dissidents. Byford (2011), in fact, claims that CTs remain the refuge of every dictator and authoritarian leader in the world. Still, it is noteworthy how CTs have in contemporary western democracies spread widely as political tool.

This trend turns conspiracy theorists away from the fringe and the underprivileged. In a way, this leads to a process of mainstreaming the margins. When upheld by the powerful, previously discredited CTs enter into a process of legitimatization and, thus, pose a threat to the liberal political system stemming from the very power centres themselves.

The Red Scare in the USA, and subsequent McCarthyism in the 1950s, is an example of how political elites can manipulate popular fears in society and feed them. US authorities were actively engaged in political fear mongering, implying an imminent threat of communist infiltration in the USA, a process which they claimed had, by then, already reached the very upper echelons of society. In his study, Richard Hofstadter took both McCarthyism and the conservative politics of Republican presidential candidate, Barry Goldwater, as examples of populism and what he coined as the paranoid style of American politics.

Conspiracy theories upheld by elite and authorities take many forms. Here is one example. In January 2012, the National Committee of the Republican party in the USA issued a resolution denouncing so-called Agenda 21, saying it was a 'destructive and insidious scheme' that would impose a 'socialist/communist redistribution of wealth' (Potok and Terry 2015a). This was an echo of what, for example, the John Birch Society had warned against, which insisted that Agenda 21 was aimed at ending freedom and American sovereignty in the name of environmentalism. Insisting that it would bring 'new Dark Ages of pain and misery yet unknown to mankind,' The Birch Society furthermore claimed that it would 'make our nation a vassal of the UN' (ibid.). This surely sounds serious, and if correct, the Republicans would have been right in warning against such devastation. The only problem was, however, that there was no truth to it.

In reality, Agenda 21 was a nonbinding plan promoting sustainability of natural resources. It was issued by the UN and signed at the Rio Earth Summit in 1992 by the leaders of 178 countries, including Republican US President George H.W. Bush.

Many studies indicate that politicians and activists often deliberately use CTs to spread fear and distrust in society. Most recently, this has been done via fake news and what can be understood as the politics of misinformation. Karen Douglas (2017), for example, argues that the way US President Donald Trump systemically applied those CTs that easily resonated with suspicions voters already hold, suggests that he was promoting them deliberately for his political gain.

Populist actors in politics often position themselves as the true defenders of the people, heroically standing against an external threat. Simultaneously, they point a finger at others in the domestic elite who they accuse of having betrayed the public. This is the process of identifying enemies of the people. In Turkey, for instance, several CTs have been offered by President Recep Erdogan's regime, implicating foreign actors in a plot against the Turkish nation. Another example includes the ultranationalist Polish ruling party, Law and Justice, who had concocted stories of Poland's post-communist leaders plotting with a clan of old communists to return the country under a totalitarian order (*The Economist* 2016).

A similar sort of rhetoric has also been commonly used by, for example, Vladimir Putin in Russia, Marine Le Pen in France and, indeed, Donald Trump and the Tea Party in the US. These leaders have been found to uphold a rhetorical division of *Us* versus *Them*—all discussed further in following segments.

The National Front in France

The far-right Front National in France, founded by Jean Marie Le Pen in 1973, offers a good example of how populists weave CTs into their political discourse. By entangling CTs and populism in their rhetoric, the party aligned the *corrupt elite* with the alleged *conspirators* and the *pure people* with the *unknowing*, i.e. the *victimised*.

This is amongst conclusions of a string of French scholars—i.e. Cuminal et al. (1997), Guland (2000) and Jamin (2009)—who have analysed how both strands: populism and CTs, have culminated in the politics of the FN. These French scholars illustrate how the FN attacks the establishment but does not seek to overthrow the democratic system. Rather, the party advocated ousting of the elite and instating a better democratic system *of* the common people and *for* the common people.

Conspiracy theories upheld by the FN have been of several kinds and have evolved over time. During the Cold War, prior to the collapse of the Berlin wall, the FN aimed to unravel a 'grand communist conspiracy to influence the world' (Hauwaert 2012)—for example, through the UN where communists, they insisted, were manipulating events behind the scenes. The FN warned against communists infiltrating many international organizations. In addition to the UN, the EU and even NATO—sometimes in league with Jews—were seen as facades for a communist led New World Order (ibid.). On these grounds, the FN opposed internationalization of France and was able to accuse the domestic elite of being entangled in a global cabal of evil-doers.

The FN weaved CTs into its populist rhetoric from the outset. Although often aiming to unravel these kinds of external threats, its principal political focus was still firmly focused on the French establishment (Hauwaert 2012). Positioning themselves on the outside of French politics, they accused the elite of being corrupt and collectively engaging in covert manipulations across party lines. Here, the FN also accused the mainstream in French politics of being accomplices of the foreign conspirators and, thus, of betraying the ordinary people in France into the hands of external evil.

After the FN did worse than expected in the 2015 local elections, Marine Le Pen—who had succeeded her father as party leader—blamed 'the regime', i.e. the French mainstream elite, which had 'conspired to block her rise' (cited in Nougayrede 2015). She claimed that her opponents had collectively colluded in order to hinder the will of the people to materialize, in other words; her own advancement—which here is entangled into one. In this discursive creation, she is portrayed as the good representative of the people, heroically fighting the malignant elite who is turned into an opponent of the pure people.

The FN is a good example of how right-wing nationalist populists apply CTs to discursively turn the mainstream political elite into traitors and, thus, enemies of the people. The party started out in fighting a communist conspiracy, but since moved on to unpack a kind of New World Order-type globalist covert conspiracy led by NATO, EU, UN, IMF and the wider international financial establishment. Later, the FN turned their focus much more firmly on immigration and on opposing what they saw as Islamist infiltration, which is the subject of analysis in Chapter 6.

Post-Soviet Russia

Conspiracy theories have always been a prevalent feature in Russian culture. Throughout Soviet times, anti-Jewish CTs were, for example, upheld in national patriotic literature and also promoted by even the communist party (Yablokov 2018). With the dissolution of the Soviet Union in 1991, an avalanche of nationalistic sentiments overtook Russia, where ultra-nationalists took to distributing mostly anti-Western CTs.

Anxiety and feelings of powerlessness in post-Soviet Russia proved to be a fertile breeding ground for CTs. This led to a growing nostalgia of past Soviet times and simultaneous a rise in anti-Western attitudes. Ilya Yablokov (2018), illustrates how anti-Western CTs framed the nation-building discourse in Putin's Russia and that by doing so, the strong leader was able to suppress dissident voices.

In Russia, the West was treated as the ultimate other who was seeking to prevent Russia from flourishing. Studies have shown that most actors in Russian politics have applied this notion in one way or another. Yablokov (2014) shows how anti-Western CTs were used by Russian authorities. That they helped to reinforce notions of Russia as being different from the West and, secondly, that they also underlined Russia's greatness, which—vitally for the story—the West was aiming at destroying.

Russia turned heavily conspiratorial in the post-Soviet era. Perhaps apart from North Korea, CTs have in recent years become most prevalent in Russia where post-truth politics (see further in Chapter 7) have indeed reached new heights. The Russian state media has played a pivotal role in this turn. In the Ukrainian conflict they, for example, ran a series of fabricated stories claiming that pro-Western authorities in Kiev were crucifying children (*The Economist* 2016).

Russia Today (RT), the Moscow based state controlled English language 24-hour television news station, opened its doors to a global creed of CTs, welcoming almost anyone with a story undermining the credibility of the West on its airwaves to voice their suspicions. Their contributors, for example, included Alex Jones and Jim Marrs discussed before. RT presenters would seriously discuss covert actions of the Bilderberg group, 9/11 truther's theories, and stories of climate change conspiracies, treating them as credible news stories (Byford 2011).

Collectively, this constitutes a systemic campaign of misinformation upheld by the authorities themselves. Accordingly, Peter Pomerantsev's (2015) unauthorised biography of Russian President Vladimir Putin was titled *Nothing Is True and Everything Is Possible*. These far-fetched CTs of aggressive outsiders were actively promoted by Putin and his clan for their political gain domestically. As *Guardian* columnist Natalie Nougayrede (2015) writes, this rhetoric centres on the notion that western powers were engaged in covert manipulations with the intent of ultimately 'dismantling the very statehood of Russia.'

This discursive creation of external plots also serves to manipulate groups within Russia. By portraying domestic dissidents as covert aggressors from abroad, the Russian state not only claimed the right to crush nonconformist voices within Russia, but also insisted that it was obliged to do so. Taking them on at home was, thus, part of the good fight against foreign enemies.

This discursive construction, furthermore, provided authorities with a means to be able to blame almost anything that goes wrong at home on the external enemy and its covert domestic collaborators. Vladimir Putin, for example, repeatedly, or perhaps rather continuously, put up a fight against what he perceived as a US led world order aimed against Russia, which he claimed had the aim of ruining Russia.

This is a clear example of how a CT of a foreign plot was systematically used domestically by a populist who placed himself as a protector of the nation against a foreign threat, which he himself had discursively created in the minds of the domestic people. By applying this simplistic dualist world-view, he could also turn against any disobedient voices domestically, as they could simply be branded as traitors of the people in the good fight.

Here, the leader equates himself with the people against both external threats and domestic traitors. Discursively, the people and their leader become a single entity. This is similar to what, for example, Donald Trump attempted in the USA, by branding the media as enemies of the people, which I turn to in the next segment.

As here has been discussed, fear of Western subversion became a key instrument for social cohesion of the Russian nation. Gradually, there was, though, a shift from fears of Western forces as the primary threat to Russia, towards also including fears of migrants. This turned into an evolving belief in a migrant conspiracy, that external forces were now also plotting to ruin Russian society by migrant infiltration (Yablokov 2018). Another source of widespread CTs in Russia came to revolve around the malcontent feminist Punk Rock band, Pussy Riot, which I discuss further in Chapter 7, as well as the many fake news stories coming out of Russia.

Before leaving Russia here, we should though clearly note, that many anti-Russian CTs have also, for a long time, been floating around in the West. The relationship between Russia and the West, in this regard, is not a one-way street. During the Cold War, Russia was, indeed, also seen as the arch enemy of the West. The Soviet Union was widely viewed as a conspiring state, using various demonic means in advancing its communist cause. The Cold War created a sustained and prolonged *Manichean* moral order in the West (Barkun 2013). On both sides, this was indeed treated as a continuous battle between *light* and *darkness*, *good* and *evil*.

The end of communism and dissolution of the Soviet Union deprived the West of its archetypical *Other*, the collective enemy which the West had unified against. Some of these suspicions have since filtered over onto post-Soviet Russia. Western media has, for example, been filled with stories of Putin's clan in the Kremlin supporting disruptive forces variously in the West, such as funding the Front National in France and other far-right parties in Europe. This has, for instance, led many to suspect these parties of being Putin's Trojan horses in the European Union.

Many stories have also been reported of covert operations of Russian authorities deliberately aimed at disrupting the liberal democratic order in the West (Mudde 2016). These have included reports of Russians interfering in the US 2016 presidential election and the following year in the Catalonia separatist campaign in Spain. Also, many reports have been floating around about the Russian state assassinating people in the West. Some of these stories have since been proven correct; others only to have had a grain of truth to them, while many were overtly exaggerated. Interestingly, for the discussion here, mere fabrications have also been thrown into the mix, fuelled primarily by long-lasting fears of Russia in the West.

Trump's America

In the US presidential campaign of 2016, populism and conspiratorialism rose to new heights in American politics, culminating with the election of Donald Trump to the oval office. The fact checking site, *PolitiFact*, found more of Mr. Trumps statements to have been 'absolutely false' than of any other candidate in the race (*The Economist* 2016). He, for example, upheld bogus claims of diverse topics such as Obama's birth place, climate change and immigration. A *New York Times* study found that in Trump's first ten months in office, he told 103 separate untruths, many of them repeatedly. Comparing that with his predecessor, Barack Obama, reveals the astounding comparison, as Obama was found to have told 18 untruths over his entire eight-year tenure. This equates to an average of about two a year for Obama and a staggering 124 a year for Trump (Leonhardt et al. 2017).

By fuelling the previously discussed so-called Birther movement, suspecting Barack Obama of being foreign born, and, thus, not legitimate as US president, Trump and other conspiratorialists inserted doubts about his Americanness. Instead, the US President was cast as foreign, and un-American. In other words, this was the process of *othering* even the sitting US President. In many communications, Trump claimed that climate change was a Chinese plot, designed to damage the US economy (Aistrope 2016).

When kicking off his campaign, Trump set the tone by vilifying Mexican immigrants who he linked to rapes and the US drug problem (Potok 2017). He, for instance, retweeted a message by a white suprem- acist who falsely claimed that blacks were responsible for 80 percent of murders of white people in America (ibid.). He also wrongly insisted that inner city crime was at a record high (*The Economist* 2016).

Donald Trump even went so far as implying that Barack Obama was the founder of the Muslim terrorist organisation Isis. Although admit- ting that Obama might not himself have physically established the organization, he still insisted that Obama had been the most valuable player in their formation: 'I give him the most valuable player award.' Trump moved on to also implicate his rival in the presidential election with the founding of Isis: 'I give her, too, by the way, Hillary Clinton.' When criticised for implicating Obama (without merit) with the noto- rious terrorist organization, Trump reiterated his claim: 'I don't care. He was the founder. The way he got out of Iraq was, that was the founding of Isis. Ok?' (*The Economist* 2016).

Illustrative of how populism advances through the ranks in politics, the racist radical-right in America sincerely celebrated Trumps election. Andrew Anglin, founder of the neo-Nazi website, *Daily Stormer*— named after the German Nazi propaganda gutter press known as *Der Stürmer*—for example, wrote: 'We won, brothers. All of our work. It has paid off. Our Glorious Leader has ascended to God Emperor. Make no mistake about it: we did this.' He went on writing: 'All my friends in Europe are texting me "NOW WE'RE GOING TO GET TO KICK OUT THESE MONKEYS!!!!".' In conclusion he wrote that '…the White race is back in the game' (cited in Ennis 2016). White suprem- acist Richard Spencer said that Trump's election marked a victory for identity politics (Potok 2017). This is significant, as promoting identity is indeed the core to nationalist populism.

Many further comments of Donald Trump and his supporters demonstrate the turn to populism and conspiratorialism. Content anal- ysis of his speeches and other communications, conducted by Oliver and Rahn (2016), indicate that Trump was more than any other can- didate prone to apply rhetoric that was 'distinctive in its simplicity, anti-elitism and collectivism.' When studying some of these statements, it seems that Mr. Trump did not care much whether his words were true or not. For instance, at a fundraising speech in March 2018, he boasted that in a meeting with Canadian Prime Minister, Justin Trudeau, he had, without knowing the facts, made up information, insisting that the US ran a trade deficit with its northern neighbour (Dawsey et al. 2018).

Perhaps, thus, Trump is the archetypical example of a *Post-Truth* politician, which is further discussed in Chapter 7. Oliver and Rahn (ibid.) also found that Trump's supporters were 'distinctive in their high level of conspiratorial thinking, nativism and economic insecurity.'

Last, I turn to anti-EU CTs and the Brexit campaign in the UK.

Brexit and Anti-EU

The European Union has long been a target of many conspiracy theorists. Suspicions around European integration being an instrument for a New World Order have been widespread. I have previously mentioned the notion of the EU being a resurrected Roman Empire, this time, for instance, as a super-state led by the Antichrist. In one version, the institution itself is seen as the Antichrist, more specifically, taking on the formation of a computer hiding deep within the European institutional apparatus in Brussels, keeping track of everyone in the world (Boyer 1995). In Europe, well-paid EU officials have increasingly become culprits in many tales of this sort of a malignant order. In the story, they most often serve as domestic traitor, while immigrants—mainly Muslims and some other minorities—are depicted as dangerous others.

The literature claiming to unravel EU related conspiracies is vast. In his book titled *The Dark Modern Age—A Farewell to the Enlightenment*, Hungarian Janos Drabik (2017) for instance, writes that the EU 'is the institute of the plutocratic world-elite.' He insists that the EU was not constructed for the people of Europe, 'but by the world-ruling elite. It is the transnational monetary cartel holding power over states that wants to get rid of national states by all means.' Drabik moves on to insist that the 'world-ruling elite has gradually annihilated the achievements of the Enlightenment', and that the global system is 'controlled from one single centre.'

These are some of the more severe anti-EU CTs. As was discussed at the beginning of this chapter there were also several softer CTs floating around in the debate prior to the Brexit vote in the UK, held on 23 June 2016.

'Let's give the NHS the £350 million the EU takes every week' (Bennett 2016). This was the message on the first billboard of the Vote Leave campaign published on 15 April 2016—unequivocally insisting not only that EU membership cost the UK this vast sum of money every week, but also that the enormous amount would be available to fund the UK National Health Service after leaving. The same message was printed widely in Brexit campaign materials, famously, for example, on the side of their campaign buses. At best, this was very misleading. Not only was this a gross figure, blown out of all proportion and without taking into account returns through EU programs, but also it not even deduct the so-called UK rebate,[1] adding to the calculation amounts that never even left Britain.

Portraying their message in this way fits with classic populist positioning, like the ones discussed in Chapter 4. Here, EU membership is linked to the NHS being underfunded. In other words, this is a classic false opposition, where funding the NHS properly is directly linked with leaving the EU. Furthermore, this serves to oppose *us* with *them*, protecting *our* NHS against paying into the *foreign* EU. By their positioning, the EU was placed as a threat to proper healthcare in Britain.

When criticised by many specialists for his simplistic and antagonistic protrusion of the situation, a leading Brexit campaigner of the Conservative Party, Michael Gove, replied saying: 'I think the people in this country have had enough of experts' (cited in Bennett 2016).

Taking back money was but one of many messages that were only loosely linked to reality. Leading up to a visit by US President Barack Obama, who was expected to come out against Brexit and say that in the case of a leave vote, it would take a long time to negotiate a trade deal between the USA and the UK, many of the Brexiters took to undermining the US president's credibility. Writing in the tabloid, the *Sun* ahead of the visit, then London Mayor, Boris Johnson, for instance, said that due to his part Kenyan ancestry, Obama had a dislike of the British Empire. To underpin the claim, Johnson insisted that Obama had, because of that reason, removed a bust of Winston Churchill from the Oval Office in Washington, upon taking office as US President. After Johnson was criticised for covert dog whistle racism, UKIP leader Nigel Farage came to his defence. Farage wrote that Obama indeed 'bears a bit of grudge against this country because of his grandfather and Kenya and colonialization' (cited in Bennett 2016).

When in London, Obama confirmed that on a possible trade deal 'The UK is going to be in the back of the queue.' In responding to Obama, Nigel Farage focused on the wording rather than on the content of the message. He voiced suspicion of the American using the word *queue* rather than *line*. The UKIP leader detected a conspiracy in the US President's wording, implying that the speech had been written by a Brit, and, indeed drafted by Downing street. On BBC Radio 4, Farage insisted that 'no American would say "back of the queue"… Americans use the world "line"' (cited in Bennett 2016).

Another conspiratorial aspect in the Brexit campaign was related to fears of possible access of Turkey to the EU and, thus, of increased Muslim migration to the UK. I discuss this further in the next chapter dealing with anti-Muslim CTs, the fear of Islamist takeover of Europe— which recently has turned into an immense and rapidly developing CT.

Note

1. The UK rebate, sometimes called the UK correction, is a specific calculation conducted since 1985 that reduces Britain's contribution to the EU budget. The main argument for it was that the UK would otherwise overtly pay for agricultural subsidies elsewhere in the union.

References

Aistrope, T. (2016). *Conspiracy theory and American foreign policy*. Manchester: Manchester University Press.
Barkun, M. (2013). *A culture of conspiracy: Apocalyptic visions in contemporary America*. Berkeley: University of California Press.

Bartlett, J., & Miller, C. (2010). *The power of unreason: Conspiracy theories, extremism and counter-terrorism*. London: Demos. Retrieved from western-voice.net.

Bennett, O. (2016). *The Brexit club: The inside story of the leave campaign's shock victory*. London: Biteback Publishing.

Booth, R., Dodd, V., Rawlinson, K., & Slawson, N. (2016, June 18). Jo Cox murder suspect tells court his name is "death to traitors, freedom for Britain". *The Guardian*. London.

Boyer, P. (1995). *When time shall be no more: Prophecy belief in modern American culture*. Cambridge: Harvard University Press.

Byford, J. (2011). *Conspiracy theories: A critical introduction*. Basingstoke: Palgrave Macmillan.

Cheminade, J. (1984). Mitterrand joins Soviet offensive to destroy France and the Western alliance. *Executive Intelligence Review, 11*(49), 40–42.

Cheminade, J. (1996). Time to destroy the mythology of Bonapartism. *The Executive Intelligence Review, 23*(42), 18–41.

Cheminade, J. (2000). FDR and Jean Monnet: The Battle vs. British Imperial Methods can be won. *Executive Intelligence Review, 27*(24), 44–55.

Cobain, I., & Taylor, M. (2016, November 23). Far-right terrorist Thomas Mair jailed for life for Jo Cox murder. *The Guardian*. London.

Cobain, I., Parveen, N., & Taylor, M. (2016, November 23). The slow-burning hatred that led Thomas Mair to murder Jo Cox. *The Guardian*. London.

Cuminal, I., Souchard, M., Wahnich, S., & Wathier, V. (1997). *Le Pen, les mots. Analyse d'un discours d'extrême-droite*. La Découverte: Paris.

Dawsay, J., Paletta, D., & Werner, E. (2018, 14 March). In fundraising speech, Trump says he made up trade claim in meeting with Justin Trudeau. *The Washington Post*. Washington, DC.

Douglas, K. (2017). You just can't trust 'em. *International Politics and Society*. Brussels. Retrieved from ips-journal.eu.

Douglas, K., Sutton, R., & Cichocka, A. (2017). The psychology of conspiracy theories. *Current Directions in Psychological Science, 26*, 538–542. https://doi.org/10.1177/0963721417718261.

Drabik, J. (2017). *The dark modern age: A farewell to the enlightenment*. Winnipeg: Gold Book.

Ennis, D. (2016, November 11). Who's happy Trump won? The Klan, Nazis and anti-immigrant activists worldwide. *LGBTQ Nation*. Retrieved from lgbtqnation.com.

Fenster, M. (1999). *Conspiracy theories: Secrecy and power in American culture.* Minneapolis: Univeristy of Minnesota Press.

Guland, O. (2000). *Le Pen, Mégret et les juifs: l'obsession du'complot mondialiste'.* Paris: La Découverte.

Hauwaert, S. (2012). Shared dualisms: On populism and conspiracy theory. *Counterpoint.* London. Retrieved from counterpoint.uk.com.

Imhoff, R., & Bruder, M. (2014). Speaking (un-)truth to power: Conspiracy mentality as a generalised political attitude. *European Journal of Personality, 28*(1), 25–43. https://doi.org/10.1002/per.1930.

Jamin, J. (2009). *L'imaginaire du complot: discours d'extrême droite en France et aux Etats-Unis.* Amsterdam: Amsterdam University Press.

Jo Cox murder: Judge's sentencing remarks to Thomas Mair. (2016, November 23). London. BBC.com.

Leonhardt, D., Philbrick, I., & Tompson, S. (2017, December 14). Trump's Lies vs. Obama's. *The New York Times.* New York.

Machiavelli, N. (1550). *The prince.* Rome: Antonio Blado d'Asola.

Madisson, M. L. (2016). *The semiotic construction of identities in hypermedia environments: The analysis of online communication of the Estonian extreme right.* Tartu: University of Tartu Press.

Mudde, C. (2016). *On extremism and democracy in Europe.* Abingdon-on-Thames: Routledge.

Nougayrede, N. (2015, December 18). The conspiracy theories of extreme right and far left threaten democracy. *The Guardian.* London.

Oliver, J. E., & Rahn, W. M. (2016). Rise of the Trumpenvolk: Populism in the 2016 election. *The ANNALS of the American Academy of Political and Social Science, 667*(1), 189–206.

Pomerantsev, P. (2015). *Nothing is true and everything is possible: The surreal heart of the New Russia.* New York: PublicAffairs.

Popper, K. S. (2002 [1945]). *The open society and its enemies.* Abingdon-on-Thames: Routledge.

Potok, M. (2017). The year in hate and extremism. *Intelligence Report Magazine.* Montgomery: Southern Poverty Law Center. Retrieved from splcenter.org.

Potok, M., & Terry, D. (2015a). *10 right-wing conspiracy theories that have slowly invaded American politics.* Salon. Retrieved from salon.com.

Potok, M., & Terry, D. (2015b). Margins to the mainstream. *Intelligence Report Magazine.* Montgomery: Southern Poverty Law Center. Retrieved from splcenter.org.

van Prooijen, J.-W., Krouwel, A. P. M., & Pollet, T. V. (2015). Political extremism predicts belief in conspiracy theories. *Social Psychological and Personality Science, 6*(5), 570–578.

Uscinski, J. E., & Parent, J. M. (2014). *American conspiracy theories.* Oxford: Oxford University Press.

Yablokov, I. (2014). Pussy Riot as agent provocateur: conspiracy theories and the media construction of nation in Putin's Russia. Routledge. *Nationalist Papers 42*(4), 622–636.

Yablokov, I. (2018). *Fortress Russia: Conspiracy theories in the post-Soviet world.* Cambridge: Polity Press.

Yes, I'd lie to you. (2016, September 10). London. Economist.com.

6

The Eurabia Doctrine

'Our population is being replaced. No more.' These words were written by Geert Wilders (2017) leader of The Netherlands' far-right Freedom Party, when linking on Twitter to a video clip showing Muslims dominating the streets in Amsterdam. The video was titled 'Is this Iran or Pakistan? No, this is Amsterdam, the Netherlands.' This is but one example of many similar moves made by several leaders of nationalist populist parties in Europe indicating that Europe was facing a hostile takeover by Muslims.

Here is another. In the midst of the Syrian migration crisis, in March 2015, Marine Le Pen of the French National Front wrote on Twitter that France was under migratory submersion and invited her followers to read Jean Raspail's novel, *The Camp of the Saints* (*Le Camp des Saints*), published in 1994 [1974]. The book illustrates the demise of Western civilization through mass immigration from India. Biological race is here a key factor in explaining the fates of societies. Previously, Le Pen had said that the book painted a picture of a Europe being invaded by hordes of 'stinking' dark-skinned migrants and 'rat people' flowing in a 'river of sperm' (cited in Symons 2017).

© The Author(s) 2018
E. Bergmann, *Conspiracy & Populism*, https://doi.org/10.1007/978-3-319-90359-0_6

Over in America, Breitbart news editor and key advisor to Donald Trump, Steve Bannon, accepted Le Pen's invitation and started aggressively marketing the book leading up to the US 2016 presidential election. Both Bannon and Le Pen saw the story as a prophecy, that Muslim refugees were now starting an invasion of Europe. Referring to Syrian refugees in October 2015, Bannon said: 'It's been almost a Camp of the Saints-type invasion' (ibid.).

This anti-Muslim rhetoric has also been mirrored by US President Donald Trump, for instance, when retweeting three unsubstantiated anti-Muslim videos posted by British far-right activist, Jayda Fransen (see Weaver and Jacobs 2017). One of them showed a Muslim destroying a statue of the Virgin Mary, another a group of Muslims pushing a boy off a roof, and third indicated that a Muslim was hitting a Dutch boy on crutches.

A milder example, though, of a similar kind, occurred leading up to the September 2017 parliamentary election in Norway when integration minister, Sylvi Lishaug, was for several days, able to let almost the entire political debate in the country revolve around her planned trip to neighbouring Sweden, to the Stockholm suburb of Rinkeby. Her party, the nationalist populist Progress Party (*Fremskrittspartiet*—FrP), had entered government four years earlier. Seeing falling support ahead of the election, she played out the one card that was most likely to turn the tide for her party—the anti-Muslim card.

In front of the media cameras, the minister for integration warned against a lenient immigration policy as in the neighbouring state. Calling them 'no-go zones' Listhaug told tales of 'parallel societies having developed in more than 60 places in Sweden.' In these no-go places, she said, were 'a large quantity of people with immigrant backgrounds.' She insisted that they festered with 'conditions of lawlessness and criminals in control' (cited in The Local 2017).

Listhaug repeatedly warned against a foreign policy she referred to as the 'Swedish condition.' The *Financial Times* wrote that the term was code for 'gang warfare, shootings, car burnings and other integration problems' in the neighbouring country (Milne 2017). Listhaug's Swedish counterpart, Helene Fritzon, who initially had agreed to accompany the Norwegian minister on her travels, cancelled the planned visit, calling it out as merely a political stunt in the domestic election campaign. Fritzon dismissed Listhaug's description of this alleged Swedish condition as 'complete nonsense.'

Although Listhaug's act was heavily criticised across the board, both by almost the entire political class in Sweden as well as by most parties in Norway, that did not cause her to suffer at the polls. On the contrary, and even though her claims were frequently debunked by referring to established knowledge regarding integration in Sweden, her party only rose in opinion polls in the wake of the controversy. After re-winning her seat in parliament, she upheld similar rhetoric, and for example, posted on Facebook in March 2018, accusations that the Labour Party put the rights of terrorists above national security.

In this chapter, I explore the CT of an Islamist takeover of Europe, a theory which can be referred to as the *Eurabia* doctrine—the Islamization of Europe.

Migration

In the 1960s and early 1970s, workers from North Africa and the Middle East were invited to Western Europe to help rebuild the continent after the devastations of two world wars. The economy was booming and there seemed to be an endless need on the continent for fresh pairs of working hands. Amongst the migrants were many Muslims and, as a result, Europe was fast becoming multicultural.

In the wake of the oil crisis hitting hard in 1972 and the following economic slowdown, many Europeans turned critical against the influx of migrant workers from foreign lands. As was discussed in Chapter 4, populist parties were popping up in many countries of the continent at the time, positioning themselves specifically against immigrants, mainly Muslims. Europe entered into a new period of troubled religious and race relations.

Recent years have seen increased clashes between Islam and the West, for example, in repeated military invasions of Western forces in the Middle-East and frequent terrorist attacks of Islamist organizations in the West. The most severe terrorist incident came with the Al-Qaida attacks on 11 September 2001 in the USA. Recently, the terrorist organization *Isis* has been behind many terrible attacks in Western Europe, such as the massacre in the Bataclan concert hall in Paris on 13 November 2015, where 90 people were killed. These clashes have led to increasingly troubled relations between Islam and the West.

Tensions rose to new heights with the migration crisis peaking in 2015 and 2016. In the wake of the conflicts in Syria and other countries in the Middle East and North Africa, Europe saw a sudden increased influx of Muslim refugees coming in large numbers to the continent. In 2017, Muslims accounted for around five percent of the population in the European Union. An estimation of the Pew Research Centre (2017) indicates that by the year 2050, Muslims are projected to rise to between 7.4 and 14% of the population. Many of these people are, however, expected to move away from their traditional Muslim heritage and integrate into the contemporary European lifestyle.

These changes in the demographic construction of the continent have led right-wing populists in Europe to move away from anti-Semitic CTs of former times and to centre on a covert Islamist plot of taking over control in Europe, which I turn to next.

Sharia Panic

In his analysis of right-wing populists in Europe, Cas Mudde (2016) illustrates how immigrants were commonly depicted as external threats to the benign native society while the domestic elite was accused of betraying the good ordinary people. From this viewpoint, Muslims were generally portrayed as a homogeneous group of violent and authoritative religious fundamentalists, who were pre-modern and primarily anti-Western in their politics.

Chris Allen (2010) defines islamophobia in Western societies as the negative positioning of Islam and Muslims as the *Other*, posing a threat to *Us*. The archetypical Muslim in a Western depiction is, indeed, not only portrayed as inferior, but also as being alien. Anti-Muslim sentiments of this kind have become normalised in the West, and, as

Douglas Pratt and Rachel Woodlock (2017) argue, it is now woven into 'Western consciousness that Islam and Muslims pose a threat' to the Western way of life.

Anti-Muslim sentiments have, indeed, largely become legitimate in the West. Catarina Kinnvall and Paul Nesbit-Larking (2010) argue that Muslims are frequently 'featured as invaders,' often viewed as part of a 'coordinated plan to conquer Europe.' The popularity of this idea was partly due to, for example, the work of a deeply controversial French philosopher, Renaud Camus, titled the *Great Replacement* (see Finkielkraut 2017). Camus argued that European civilization and identity were at risk of being subsumed by mass migration, especially from Muslim countries, and low birth rates among the native French people. This notion of replacement, or of white genocide, has echoed throughout the rhetoric of many anti-migrant far-right movements in the West—such as by neo-racist protestors in Charlottesville in the USA in 2017, as will be discussed later in this chapter.

This fear of subversion in Europe has been pushed by many movements of right-wing populists who have, for example, applied the concept of Islamofascism as a tool to trigger a response to Muslim migration (Butter and Reinkowski 2014). Noticeably, this is generally applied to all Muslims, irrespective of whether or not they are religious or at all in support of Islamization in the West. This is an apocalyptic view of Muslims dominating and destroying the liberal and democratic Europe. In return, those that advocated for the multiculturalism and peaceful coexistence of Muslim immigrants and native Europeans were accused of naivety and betrayal (see for example Jespersen et al. 2008).

Several influential publications have been written warning of the Islamist conspiracy of occupying the West. In his book *While Europe Slept—How Radical Islam Is Destroying the West from Within*, American writer Bruce Bawer (2007) describes his feelings when arriving in Amsterdam in 1997. Bawer—who later settled in Norway—felt that he had found the closest thing to heaven on Earth, that he was finally able to escape the American Protestant fundamentalism. The book describes how he watched Western Europe gradually fallen prey to another and much more alarming fundamentalism, to Islam. In a tale of external replacement, Bawer insists that the ever so tolerant Europeans were being invaded by intolerant Muslims.

Another immensely influential book of this sort is titled *Eurabia— The Euro-Arab Axis*. Writing under the pen name Bat Ye'or (2005), its author argues that a secret war of subversion in Europe was being waged—more specifically, that a particular French group in politics and media were already well on the way to handing the continent over to Muslims. The author argues that ever since the 1973 oil crisis, the EU has been secretly conspiring with the Arab League to bring about a *Eurabia* on the continent.

Another title, *The Force of Reason* by Oriana Fallaci (2006), picked up on Ye-or's arguments and claimed that Muslims were, in fact, invading and subjugating Western Europe through a combination of immigration and fertility. She insisted that they 'have orders to breed like rats' and claimed that these 'eternal invaders rule us already.' She concluded that this was the 'biggest conspiracy that modern history has created.'

For a while now, many populist political leaders in Europe have promoted this theory, for example by nurturing the myth that migrants—especially Muslims—were taking over *our* national soil and heritage. Senior editor at the *Atlantic* magazine, Adam Serwer (2011), identified a CT he called the Sharia panic in America, the fear of American Muslims trying to undermine the US constitution and planning to overthrow the government. Another version insisted that Muslim terrorists were hiding in between 22 and 35 secret training camps around America (Potok and Terry 2015).

A flipside to anti-Muslim CTs in the West, was the abundance of CTs existing widely in the Arab world. Matthew Gray (2010) claims that CTs were a 'salient feature of the political discourses' in the Arab Middle East. He insisted that to understand the politics of the region, it was vital to understand its 'conspiracism.' Amongst the most salient CTs in the Arab world were those of Zionist plots to take over control in the region. Another theme revolved around tales of the West waging all-out war on Islam. Next, I turn to discussing specific cases of anti-Muslim CTs in the West, starting with the Brexit debate in the UK.

Brexit—Fear of Muslim Migration

In the preceding chapter, I discussed conspiratorial aspects detected in the 2016 Brexit campaign in the UK. Here, I focus on anti-Muslim sentiments in that debate. The Leave campaign directly played into many people's anxiety over Turkey joining the EU. Even dismissing the fact that all EU members states hold a veto of new members, they still insisted that the UK would, in practice, not be able to stop the Turks from getting their hands on EU passports. UKIP leader, Nigel Farage, forcefully maintained that 75 million poor Turks were on the verge of gaining access to the UK, 'to use the Health Service, to use our primary schools, to take jobs in whatever sector it may be' (cited in Bennett 2016).

The UKIP leader said that the Brexit vote was indeed a referendum on the massive migration of Muslims into the UK. He went on to insist that even combatants of the terrorist organization Isis would, as well, filter through to the UK with Syrian refugees coming from Turkey. Many supported this view. In a speech promoting Farage's message, prominent Conservative Party member, Theresa Villiers, for example said: 'If people believe there is an immigration crisis today, how much more concerned will they be after free movement is given to Turkey's 75 million citizens.' Former Conservative party leader, Ian Duncan Smith, similarly insisted the EU had made it very clear that Turks 'are going to get free travel and then enter the EU.' In a statement, Vote Leave went on to state that the birth rate in Turkey would lead to a million Muslim Turks coming to the UK within eight years (Bennett 2016).

This message was actively built into campaign material of Vote Leave in the Brexit campaign. One of their posters, for example, depicted an open door to the UK with the written message: 'Turkey (population of 76 million) is joining the EU.' Another poster listed countries set to join the EU, highlighting only Syria and Iraq on the map. Neither country was, though—of course—on any kind of route towards EU membership. Still, with the focus in the campaign shifting to imagined Turkish membership and invented increased Muslim immigration into the UK, the polls started to move in the favour of Leave. A third poster showed a photograph of a seemingly endless flow of refugees crossing through the Balkans, mostly young males. The text on the poster read: 'Breaking point—the EU has failed us all.' At the bottom, the message continued: 'We must break free from the EU and take back control of our borders' (Bennett 2016). Collectively, this constitutes a systemic campaign of misinformation, which is the subject of analysis in the next chapter.

These were some of the political messages that Thomas Mair—murderer of MP Jo Cox, discussed at the beginning of previous chapter—was so susceptible to. Of course, as previously stated, the Brexit campaigners cannot be held directly accountable for Mair's actions. Still, as Alex Massie (2016) wrote in the Spectator: 'When you shout BREAKING POINT over and over again you don't get to be surprised when someone breaks.' Massie argued that when politics are presented as a matter of life and death like in the Brexit campaign, as a question of national survival, 'don't be surprised if someone takes your word for it.'

Muslim America

Relationships between the United States and many Muslim countries have been strained for a long while, evident, for example, in repeated invasions of US militaries in the Middle East, such as in the Gulf war of 1990, and in terrorist actions of Arabs in the USA. The most severe occurred on 11 September 2001 when several Al-Qaida terrorists conducted the most horrendous attack on US soil since Pearl Harbour during the Second World War. This vicious cycle was amongst what Samuel Huntington (1993, 1996) was trying to capture in his influential writings, *The Clash of Civilizations*. Huntington maintained that after the collapse of communism, Islam would emerge as the main ideological adversary of the West.

Most Americans were taken wholly by surprise on 9 November 2001. Rather than focusing on the attackers and the active plotters as individuals and as specific identifiable perpetrators, many sought explanations of why Muslims, in general, hated them. This is what can be described as an 'Arab-Muslim paranoia narrative' (Aistrope 2016).

Even prior to the 9/11 attacks, authors like Bernhard Lewis (1990) searched for 'the roots of Muslim rage' to explain hostility in the Arab world towards the USA. Lewis maintained that this hatred, at times, went beyond hostility and 'becomes a rejection of Western civilization', which, indeed, is 'seen as innately evil, and those who promote or accept them as the "enemies of God."'

This assertion, that Arabs simply hate Western values, can feel quite convenient as it dismisses any implications of American foreign policy playing a part in these sorts of counter measures.

The controversy around the planned Islamic community centre —Park51—in lower Manhattan, is illustrative of the combative attitude towards Muslims in the USA. Opposition soon rose, branding the project as the 'Ground-Zero mosque.' The leader of the opposition, Pamela Geller (2010), wrote on her blog: 'This is Islamic domination and expansionism. The location is no accident. Just as Al-Aqsa was built on top of the Temple in Jerusalem.' She claimed to be at a front line of a cultural war. 'To allow a mosque at a place a Muslim gang destroyed on 9/11 would amount to formally blessing Islam's 1400-year-old tradition of exclusivity and suppression of all persons of all other faiths. It would be a 100% victory of Islam and sharia law over the US Constitution and America's time-honored democracy and pluralism.'

As Stephanie Wright (2017) notes, this rhetoric gained wide political backing in the USA, with former Vice Presidential candidate, Sarah Palin, tweeting that the community centre would be a 'a stab in the heart' of Americans. Former speaker of Congress, Newt Gingrich, also echoed Geller warning that the mosque was a step towards replacing the US Constitution with the totalitarian supremacy 'of Sharia law,' and that the project, in effect, amounted to a case of 'cultural, political and legal jihad' (cited in Wright 2017).

President Donald Trump was also amongst the most forceful actors in generally vilifying Muslims in the USA. The tweets mentioned at the beginning of this chapter are only amongst many actions and comments the US President has made indicating his anti-Muslim views. He, for example, proposed that authorities operate a database keeping track of American Muslims. And when, in 2016, arguing for banning many Muslims from entering the USA, he said, for instance: 'I think Islam hates us' (cited in Schleifer 2016). As President, he was, in the following year, able to prevent citizens of several Muslim dominated countries from travelling to the USA.

The US President also voiced his concern regarding the Islamization of Europe, especially in the UK. In 2015, he tweeted that British authorities were disguising 'their massive Muslim problem' (cited in Walters 2015). He furthermore tweeted that more Muslims in the UK joined Isis than joined the British army. He went on to claim that parts of London and Paris were 'so radicalised' that police officers were 'afraid for their very lives.'

Donald Trump has long made false claims about Muslims. He, for example, insisted that Muslims knew in advance about the San Bernardino mass shooting in December 2015 and did not report it. Famously, he accused Muslims in New Jersey of having celebrated the terrorist attacks on 9/11. In a television interview with George Stephanopoulos on ABC News, in November 2015, Trump said that when the towers came down, he had watched on television where a heavy Arab population in New Jersey were cheering their downfall. 'Thousands and thousands of people were cheering as that building was coming down,' he said (cited in Kessler 2015). Like so many others of a similar kind, this statement was not substantiated with evidence. Surely, it has been well documented that some Arabs in the Middle East did celebrate the attack, but no evidence at all existed that Arabs in New Jersey were cheering as the towers fell.

In other words, all of these statements were untrue. Perhaps tellingly for his politics, Trump announced his plan of banning citizens from several Muslim dominated countries from entering the USA on conspiratorialist Alex Jones' radio show.

Furthermore, illustratively for the impact the Presidents' rhetoric has had on the people around him, his then National Security Advisor, Michael Flynn, for example, followed suit and tweeted that to fear Muslims was rational. Flynn went on to describe Islam as a 'malignant cancer' (cited in Potok 2017).

With these sorts of statements in mind, it is perhaps not surprising that a study of the Public Religion Research Institute (2011) in Washington found that one third of Republicans believed that Muslims wanted to instate sharia laws in the USA.

Charlottesville—White Genocide

Many examples exist of violent actions against Muslims in the West. One occurred in the US town of Charlottesville, Virginia, in 2017. In the early afternoon on Saturday August 12, 20-year-old James Alex Fields Jr of Ohio ploughed his car into a crowd of anti-racist protesters, killing a 32-year-old woman and injuring at least 19 others. The attack came in the wake of white supremacists clashing with counter demonstrators over the removal of a statue of confederate legend, General Robert E. Lee. An ultra-nationalist group called Unite the Right had organised the rally, which was described in the media as one of the largest white supremacist events in recent US history (Strickland 2017).

The protest against the removal of the statue of General Lee turned violent and gangs of white supremacists marched across the campus of the University of Virginia carrying torches and yelling slogans such as 'white lives matter' and 'blood and soil.' Another set of chants was 'You will not replace us,' followed by; 'Jews will not replace us.'

The anti-Semitic chant, here, is quite interesting as across the Atlantic, the extreme-right in Europe had recently increasingly turned their sights away from Jews and onto Muslims instead. Both paradigms, anti-Semitism and anti-Muslim sentiments, were, however, of the same nature, i.e. in casting a specifically defined out group as foreign interlopers who were to be expunged. Curiously, the American far-right activists in Charlottesville were still decorating themselves in German Nazi symbolism, such as swastikas and Hitler quotes. Amongst slogans on their posters were, 'Jews are Satan's children.' At the rally, American white supremacist leader David Duke said that 'the American media, and the American political system, and the American Federal Reserve, is dominated by a tiny minority: the Jewish Zionist cause' (Rosenberg 2017).

American anti-Semitism and anti-Muslim sentiments in Europe stem from similar fears nurtured by the far-right. Both cases cast a light on an ongoing trepidation on both sides of the Atlantic, the anxiety over the dominant people being replaced by a foreign public. The CT of a white genocide being plotted by evil external forces, and even already underway, is still alive—that Christian identity is under siege by multiculturalism and an infiltration of people of other ethnic origins.

Infiltrating the Nordics

In line with developments elsewhere in Europe, right-wing populists positioning themselves against mainly Muslim immigrants were also on the rise throughout the Nordics. In the post-war era, both Denmark and Sweden gained a reputation for being open, liberal and tolerant. The influx of foreign workers, primarily from northern Africa, the Middle East and the Balkans was growing fast in the 1960s, followed by an increased flow of refugees. Their numbers were, however, significantly lower in Finland, Iceland and Norway (Pettersen and Østby 2014).

In Denmark, the discourse on immigration drastically changed in the 1970s and 1980s, from emphasizing equal treatment and protecting human rights towards requirements of adhering to fundamental values of the native society. Denmark, indeed, proved especially fertile for cultural racism, turning densely intolerant in the 1980s. Karen Wren (2001) maintains that, paradoxically, the former liberal values in Denmark were used to legitimate negative representations of others, especially Muslims and refugees, who were discursively being construed as a threat to Danish national identity. The change started with emergence of the Progress Party (*Fremskridtspartiet*) in the early 1970s. Its leader, Mogens Glistrup, for example, once compared Muslim immigrants to a 'drop of arsenic in a glass of clear water' (cited in Wren 2001).

Silvi Listhaugs' party, discussed at the beginning of this chapter, the Norwegian Progress Party, was established around the same time and was also to turn against immigration. In the 1987 election campaign, its then leader, Carl I. Hagen, for example, quoted a letter he claimed to have received from a Muslim called Mustafa, effectively describing a conspiracy of Muslim immigrants planning to occupy Norway. This was quite remarkable as, still, Muslims accounted for only a fraction of the population. Later, the letter proved to be his own fabrication. Interestingly, after revelations that it was all a flat out lie, Hagen's party only found increasing support. Sindre Bangstad (2017) documents that for the last quarter of a century, FrP politicians have consistently cast Muslim immigrants as an external threat to Norway.

A more fundamental shift occurred in Denmark, with the rise of the Danish Peoples Party (*Dansk Folkeparti*—DF) in the 1990s, in response to increased immigration. The party firmly opposed the emergence of a multi-ethnic society. Instead it promoted homogeneity and ethno-cultural cohesion (Mouritsen and Olsen 2013). Initially, the party was widely and harshly criticized for flirting with racism. That, however, drastically changed after the terrorist attacks in the USA on 9/11. For many, the terrifying event served as a validity of the DF's criticism of Islam (Widfeldt 2015).

The DF was instrumental in the process of externalizing immigrants, and in portraying Denmark as being overrun by migrants. Their representative in the EU Parliament, Mogens Camre, for example, described Islam as an 'ideology of evil' and suggested that Muslims should be 'driven out of Western civilization' (cited in Klein 2013). He maintained that Muslim migrants couldn't successfully be integrated into Danish society and that they had, indeed, come to take over Denmark. He continued saying that all Western countries had been 'infiltrated by Muslims,' and that even though many of them spoke nicely to us, 'they are waiting to become numerous enough to get rid of us' (cited in Sommer and Aagaard 2003).

In the wake of 9/11, the 2001 parliamentary election campaign in Denmark came to revolve around immigration, and the DF surged. Ever since then, migration became perhaps the most salient issue in the country's political debate and many mainstream parties have started to toe a similar line. Gradually, a relatively widespread consensus emerged on the need to restrict immigration. In the media, immigrants and asylum seekers were negatively portrayed and xenophobia was increasing. Studies found that in covering immigration, the Danish media emphasized how it caused crime, social problems and conflict within Danish society (Stainforth 2009).

The DF was highly successful in exploiting people's fear of mainly Muslim migrants. Against a backdrop depicting a veiled woman, the party, for example, ran on the following slogan: 'Your Denmark? A multi-ethnic society with gang rapes, repression of women and gang crimes. Do you want that?' (see Klein 2013).

Welfare Chauvinism

The Nordic nationalist right separates itself from many of its counter-
parts on the European continent by emphasising protection of their
countries' vast welfare systems for the domestic population. Across the
Nordics, Muslim migrants were portrayed as a burden on the welfare
system. This can be labelled welfare chauvinism. The Norwegian FrP, for
example, argued that the welfare system needed to be shielded from the
infiltration of foreigners, who were sucking blood from it at the expense
of native Norwegians, particularly the elderly, who they vowed to protect (Jupskås 2015). The party was squarely nationalist, anti-immigrant,
specifically anti-Muslim but not openly racist. It held, by far, the most
anti-immigrant policy in the country (Rydgren 2007).

In Sweden, nationalist populists did not find significant support until
the 2010 parliamentary election when the neo-racist Sweden Democrats
(*Sverigedemokraterna*—SD) passed the electoral threshold for the first
time. In the post-war years, Sweden had emphasised openness and tolerance and multiculturalism became embedded into the social democratic
national identity. As a result, Sweden became amongst the most popular destinations for asylum seekers in Europe. When Syrian refugees
were fleeing to Europe in record numbers in 2015, most were heading
to Germany and Sweden.

The SD was able to present immigration as a threat to the vast and
all-embracing Swedish welfare system. Its leader, Jimmie Åkesson, positioned welfare and immigration as mutually exclusive and asked the
electorate to choose between the two. This was, for example, illustrated
in an SD advert in 2010: A native woman pensioner slowly moving
with her wheeled walker is overtaken by a group of fast-moving Muslim
women in burkas, who empty out the social security coffers before
the Swedish woman finally arrives. Their slogan read: 'Pensions or
immigration—the choice is yours' (cited in Klein 2013). In a traditional
welfare chauvinistic way, Åkesson and his team, thus, placed themselves
as the guardians of the welfare state, claiming that voting for immigrant
friendly mainstream parties was a vote against the traditional heritage of
Swedish welfare, while a vote for his party was for protecting the universal welfare system.

In Iceland, the Peoples Party (*Flokkur fólksins*)—elected to parliament in 2017—also upheld welfare chauvinism. For example, in a post on Facebook, party leader Inga Sæland (2016), countered the cost of asylum seekers with helping poor Icelanders. She insisted that while poor Icelanders suffered hardship, asylum seekers, upheld by the state, were living in comfort. Rhetorically she asked whether that money might instead be better used by helping poor Icelanders.

The Nordic nationalist right was especially skilful in linking other political issues to immigration, such as welfare, economy and anti-elitism (Jupskås 2015). Immigration was also directly linked to gender issues. Often DF representatives argued that Islam was incompatible with the level of women's liberation in Denmark. On those grounds, the veiling of women in Islam, for example, became a central and symbolic issue.

Ethno-Cultural Cohesion

Throughout the Nordics, nationalist populists opposed a multi-cultural state formation on ethno-cultural grounds. Anniken Hagelund (2003), for example, explained how the Norwegian FrP moved from problematizing immigration merely on economic grounds to also voicing concerns of its effect on Norway's culture. Ever since, the party has argued that in order to prevent ethnic conflict in Norway, immigration and asylum sought from 'outside the Western culture complex' had to be stemmed (cited in Hagelund 2003). This was a classic nationalist ethno-pluralist doctrine, emphasizing an importance of keeping nations separate, without openly claiming any sort of superiority. Carl I. Hagen argued that non-Western immigration would bring a culture of violence and gang mentality to Norway. These sort of concerns, about the effect of immigrants on the ethnic composition of the Nordic nations, were increasingly being voiced.

While the Norwegian FrP refused to be associated with racism, their representatives positioned themselves as brave truth-tellers, defying the political correctness of the ruling class. In 2005, they, for example, published a poster depicting a juvenile of foreign descent pointing a gun at the viewer. The text stated that 'the perpetrator is of foreign origin.' When criticized for the xenophobic undertone, the party spokesmen said that it was simply necessary to 'call a spade a spade' (Jupskås 2015).

Anders Hellstrom (2016) documents how the immigration issue gained salience in the FrP's repertoire in the 1990s, when warning against the dangers of cultural heterogeneity. In that way, the immigration issue was 'transformed from an economic to a cultural issue.' The anti-immigration rhetoric of the FrP gradually grew more distinctively anti-Muslim. Already in 1979, Carl I. Hagen described Islam as 'misanthropic and extremely dangerous religion' (cited in Jupskås 2013). Since then, the anti-Islam rhetoric of the party just continued to grow. In a report published by FrP parliamentarians in 2007, Muslim immigration was linked to terrorism, forced marriage and crime. Their rhetoric turned increasingly conspiratorial. The report for instance, identified a need to fight against Sharia laws being implemented in Muslim areas in Norway.

Similarly, in their 1989 party program (*partiprogram*), the Sweden Democrats promoted protecting Sweden as 'an ethnically and culturally homogeneous nation.' While surely moving to the mainstream, they always still firmly flagged their anti-immigrant bias. This was, for example, well-illustrated in an open letter to the Finns Party in 2015, written by the leadership of the SD's youth movement, warning their neighbour of repeating the same mistakes as had been made in Sweden. In the letter titled 'Finland, you do not want the Swedish nightmare', they said that over the decades, Sweden had been 'destroyed' by immigration, after 'undergoing an extreme transformation from a harmonious society to a shattered one.' They said that many Swedes totally opposed this system of 'mass immigration, extreme feminism, liberalism, political correctness and national self-denial.' (cited in Bergmann 2017).

Cartoon Crisis

The so-called Muhammad cartoon crisis in 2005 illustrated well the increased polarization between native Danes and immigrants in Denmark. The DF had grown stronger and its anti-immigrant politics had gained mainstream acceptance. Karen Wren (2001) argues that cultural racism in Denmark was distinctly anti-Muslim and that the DF had been successful in demonizing Muslims and, indeed, specifically portraying immigration, in general, as a Muslim invasion. In that climate, one of Denmark's largest daily newspapers, the agrarian conservative *Jyllands-Posten*, commissioned 12 editorial cartoons, most of which satirically depicted the Prophet Muhammad.

Officially, the provocation was intended to underline freedom of speech as a fundamental value in Denmark and offer a critical contribution to the debate on Islam and self-censorship. Many, however, saw it as merely being Islamophobic and racist. Most Muslims consider depicting the Prophet Muhammad in illustrations to be blasphemous and many got offended. The crisis escalated to mutual accusations and eventually led to wide-scale protests amongst Muslims in Denmark and also in a few countries in the Middle East. In Denmark, many found the aggravated response by many Muslims to validate the DF's warnings against radical Islam. In its wake, support for the party, thus, once again rose.

Dominant Discourse

A new master frame developed across many of the Nordics in which immigrants were presented as an economic burden and a cultural threat, rather than being biologically inferior. Widfeldt (2015) found that the DF's anti-immigration rhetoric revolved around three main themes: first that immigrants caused a threat to Danish culture and ethnic identity; second, as a cause of crime; and third, as a burden on the welfare state. Gradually, this understanding became a dominant political discourse on immigration and Muslims, and Denmark, in the new millennium, implemented one of the toughest immigration legislation in Western Europe.

Despite distancing itself from the Danish People's Party, the Norwegian FrP came to adopt much of their policies on immigration, for example, in cutting off foreign aid and in proposing mandatory expulsion of foreigners sentenced to jail for more than three months.

In their party action plan (*handlingsprogram*) for 2009–2013, they emphasized, for instance, much stricter rules on family reunifications, including instating the notorious Danish 24-year-old minimum rule for spouses and 18-year-old maximum rule for children.

Anders Jupskås (2015) identified five distinctive narratives that defined the anti-immigration platform of the FrP in Norway. First, that immigrants cost too much; second, that they exploited *our* welfare; third, that they were more prone to crime than the native population; fourth, that they undermined the Norwegian way of life; and lastly, that immigrants challenged Norway's values, mainly liberal values. Jupskås documented that the first two frames were present from the outset; the second two narratives emerged in the 1980s, but that the last one, regarding a challenge to liberal values, was only presented after the 9/11 terrorist attack in the USA. In any event, it is clear that the cultural emphasis in the anti-immigrant rhetoric—on rules, norms and values—only came to prominence in Norway since the 1990s. Simultaneously, the importance of the economic frames gradually decreased.

Us and Them

While avoiding being openly racist, the DF clearly made a distinction between immigrants and ethnic Danes. This discursive distinction between *others* and *us* gradually became a shared understanding across the political spectrum (Boréus 2010). The identity-based rhetoric relied on a firm moral frame in which *others* were negatively represented as inferior to *us*. Jens Rydgren (2010) defined this as a 'neo-racist rhetoric', where national values were being framed as under threat by immigration.

The DF's 2009 manifesto stated that nativity was higher amongst immigrants than amongst ethnic Danes. This suggests that the party defined Danish nationality by ethnicity. This version of nationalism, thus, combines both cultural and ethnic elements. The manifesto, for example, found a multicultural society to be one 'without inner context and cohesion' and 'burdened by lack of solidarity' and therefore 'prone to conflict' (cited in Widfeldt 2015). The presence of ethnic minorities was, here, discursively problematized and presented as a threat to a fragile homogeneous Danish culture, which in Wren's (2001) description was 'perceived as a historically rooted set of traditions now under threat from globalization, the EU, and from "alien" cultures.'

The True Finns Party (*Perussuomalaiset*—PS) found electoral success in the 2011 election in Finland, first positioned against the Eurozone bailout. Their welfare chauvinism, of first protecting native Finns but excluding others, was also argued on ethno-nationalist grounds. On this platform, a more radical and outright xenophobic faction thrived within the party. Jussi Halla-aho, who became perhaps Finland's most forceful critic of immigration and multiculturalism, led the party's anti-immigrant faction. In a highly conspiratorial rhetoric, he, for example, referred to Islam as a 'totalitarian fascist ideology' and was in 2008, accused of racial hatred, when for instance, writing this about immigration on his blog: 'Since rapes will increase in any case, the appropriate people should be raped: in other words, green-leftist do-gooders and their supporters' (cited on Yle Uutiset 2008). He went on to write that the Prophet Muhammad was a paedophile and that Islam, as a religion, sanctified paedophilia (mtv.fi 2010). The Finnish Supreme Court convicted Halla-aho in June 2012 for disturbing religious worship and for ethnic agitation (Dunne 2014).

In Sweden, the SD heavily criticized the lenient immigration policy of the mainstream parties, which they said had caused segregation, rootlessness, criminality, conflict and increased tension in society (Hellstrom 2016). They, for example, described the notorious Rosengård block complex in Malmö, and other such immigrant dominated communities, as ghettos that had become no-go areas for Swedes, areas where the police even hesitated to enter. Jimmie Åkesson (2009) implied a conspiracy in which the Social Democrats had effectively turned these places into foreign-held territories, occupied by Muslims who were the country's greatest foreign threat and had even partially introduced Sharia laws on Swedish soil. One party representative, local council member, Martin Strid, went so far as indicating that Muslims were not fully human (Aftonbladet 2017).

Ultra-Nationalists

Numerous conspiratorial far-right movements have existed in the Nordic region. Many were made up of ultra-nationalists who, for example, forcefully celebrated Norse mythology (Jupskås 2013). In Norway, these sorts of movements have been seen parading the streets and, for example, violently attacking immigrants of the east-side of central Oslo, mainly refugees from North Africa and the Middle East.

As was discussed at the beginning of this book, the most horrible and traumatic incident of the Nordic ultra-nationalist extreme-right was the terrorist attack of Anders Behring Breivik on 22 July 2011, killing 77 people in a bomb blast in the administration quarter in Oslo and in a gun massacre at the Labour Party Youth movement camp in Utøya.

Prime minister Jens Stoltenberg responded with calmness, which was captured in his pledge of more openness, more humanity and more democracy—while never being naive. Not all were happy with the elegant response. Influential critic of welfare orientated and social liberal Norway, American expat Bruce Bawer (2012), for example, wrote a book describing how the liberal left had used the Breivik massacre as a tool to silence the debate about Islam. He went so far as to accuse Labour Party supporters of being the new Quislings of Norway.[1] In Bawer's view, thus, a band of left leaning liberal elite intellectuals in politics, media and academia conspired to commit treason.

Norwegian racism usually does not accept being racist at all. Public versions had indeed surely and squarely moved away from a biological base, towards being culturally based. However, such examples still did exist, even evident at the time of the Breivik trial, such as when Roma people set up camp in Oslo. The camp suffered numerous attacks and they were, for instance, described as 'rats' and 'inhuman' (see Booth 2014).

As was discussed in introduction to this book, the Breivik attack revealed a hidden sub-culture simmering undetected on the Internet, a network of racist and Islamophobic groups around the country. Other examples of Norwegian extreme-right organizations were, for instance, the Norwegian Defence League (NDL), the Norwegian Patriots

(*Norgespatriotene*) and perhaps the most influential of them all, SIAN, which stood for Stop Islamisation of Norway. Many prominent populist and extreme-right associations also existed in Finland, some including at least semi-fascist groupings. Indeed, a few parliamentarians of the True Finns Party belonged to the xenophobic organization *Suomen Sisu*. When large masses of migrants where flocking to Europe in wake of the refugee crisis, mainly from Syria, a group calling themselves Soldiers of Odin took to patrolling the street of several Finnish towns (Rosendahl & Forsell 2016). Dressed in black jackets, decorated with Viking symbolism and the Finnish flag, they claimed to be protecting native Finns from potential violent acts of the foreigners.

Growing out of the so-called White Aryan Resistance movement that had operated in Sweden since the 1990s, a pan-Nordic neo-Nazi movement, named the Nordic Resistance Movement, was rising across the region since 2016, most strongly, though, in Sweden, Norway and Finland (Bjarnefors 2017).

Fighting Islamisation

Across the region, Nordic nationalist populist parties were able to place immigrants firmly on the political agenda. In the 2009 Norwegian parliamentary election debate, for example, immigration was by far the most discussed issue by FrP candidates, mentioned twice as often as health care, the next most frequent topic of party members (Jupskås 2013). Party leader Siv Jensen warned against what she referred to as 'sneak Islamisation' of Norway, a term that was subsequently widely used in the political debate and became the primary focus of the party in the election (cited in Jupskås 2015). She maintained that demands of the Muslim community, such as halal meat being served in schools, the right to wear a hijab and of public celebration of Muslim holidays, were all examples of such sneak Islamization.

This notion of sneak Islamization alludes to a hidden process already in place, eventually altering Norway and turning it away from its liberal Christian roots and towards becoming a Muslim-based society. This notion—or perhaps rather, this outright CT—has led some within the populist parties in the Nordic countries to promote an active and sometimes forceful resistance against this alleged alteration of the Nordic societies. It can be argued that Anders Behring Breivik was at least partially responding to this kind of rhetoric in his horrible actions: the notion of Islamization of Europe. He claimed that he was simply a soldier fighting against a Muslim conspiracy to take over Europe (Fekete 2012). As Bangstad (2017) notes, this rhetoric is strikingly similar to the one upheld in the counter jihad and anti-Eurabia movement, by writers such as Robert Spencer, who, for instance, inspired Anders Breivik. Similar to Jensen, Spencer (2008) also warned against what he called 'stealth jihad.'

An interesting example of the conspiratorial nature of the rhetoric around Muslims in Norway is found in the case of an alleged militant Pakistani milieu in Oslo. In 2005, the FrP spokesman on immigration, Per Sandberg, revealed in the tabloid newspaper, Verdens Gang (VG) that this secretive extremist Muslim network, which was 'fundamentalist, anti-democratic and potentially violent' had 30,000 members in Oslo (cited in Bangstad 2017). As Bangstad notes, despite being utterly fabricated, this suspicion spread around Norway in many uncritical media reports.

In Denmark, the DF firmly kept up its anti-immigrant rhetoric, which, for example, was illustrated in the following two examples. In a TV debate in November 2010, then party leader, Pia Kjærsgaard, suggested banning satellite dishes in immigrants' 'ghettos', because through them, Muslims in Denmark gained access to Arabic TV channels such as Al-Jazeera and Al Arabiya (Klein 2013). Another example came in the wake of the Paris terrorist attack in late 2015, where Muslim jihadists, mainly from Belgium and France, killed 129 people. When responding to the terrible attack on television, DF's foreign policy spokesman, Søren Espersen (2015), said that Western military forces should now start bombing civil targets in Syria, specifically also in areas where there were women and children.

Many similar examples of promoting confrontation also exist in Finland. Olli Immonen, a well-known PS representative, for example, posted on Facebook a photo of himself with members of the neo-Nazi extreme-right group, the Finnish Resistance Movement. Defending his actions, he wrote that he would give his life for the battle against multiculturalism. In another Facebook post (cited in Winneker 2015), Immonen said that he was 'dreaming of a strong, brave nation that will defeat this nightmare called multiculturalism. This ugly bubble that our enemies live in, will soon enough burst into a million little pieces.' He said that these were the days 'that will forever leave a mark on our nation's future. I have strong belief in my fellow fighters. We will fight until the end for our homeland and one true Finnish nation. The victory will be ours.'

Note

1. Vidkun Quisling, leader of the Norwegian interwar nationalist party, *National Samling*, was a Nazi collaborator and traitor during the German occupation of Norway in WWII. He was executed by firing squad in 1945.

References

Aistrope, T. (2016). *Conspiracy theory and American foreign policy*. Manchester: Manchester University Press.

Åkesson, J. (2009, October 19). *Muslimerna är vårt största utländska hot*. Stockholm: Aftonbladet.

Allen, C. (2010). *Islamophobia*. Farnham: Ashgate.

Bangstad, S. (2017). Norwegian right-wing discourses: Extremism post-Utøya. In Pratt & Wodlock (Eds.), *Fear of Muslims international perspectives on Islamophobia*. Cham: Springer.

Bat, Y. (2005). *Eurabia. The Euro-Arab axis*. Cranbury: Fairleigh Dickinson University Press.

Bawer, B. (2007). *While Europe slept: How radical Islam is destroying the West from within*. Norwell: Anchor Press.

Bawer, B. (2012). *The new Quislings: How the international left used the Oslo massacre to silence debate about Islam*. New York: Broadside.

Bennett, O. (2016). *The Brexit club: The inside story of the leave campaign's shock victory*. London: Biteback Publishing.

Bergmann, E. (2017). *Nordic nationalism and right-wing populist politics: Imperial relationships and national sentiments*. London: Palgrave Macmillan—Springer.

Bjarnefors, S. (2017). *Nazister vill frikännas efter bombdomarna*. Gothenburg: Göteborgs-Posten.

Booth, M. (2014). *The almost nearly perfect people: The truth about the Nordic miracle*. London: Jonathan Cabe.

Boréus, K. (2010). Including or excluding immigrants? The impact of right-wing populism in Denmark and Sweden. In B. Bengtsson, P. Strömblad, & A. H. Bay (Eds.), *Diversity, inclusion and citizenship in Scandinavia*. Newcastle-upon-Tyne: Cambridge Scholars.

Butter, M., & Reinkowski, M. (2014). Introduction: Mapping conspiracy theories in the United States and the Middle East. In Butter & Reinkowski (Eds.), *Conspiracy theories in the United States and the Middle East: A comparative approach*. Berlin: De Gryter.

Dunne, D. (2014, August 7). Finns Party MP remains defiant after race hate conviction. *Helsinki Times*. Helsinki.

Espersen, S. (2015). DF om krigen mod IS: Vi bliver nødt til at bombe civile nu—også kvinder og børn. Retrieved from politik.tv2.dk.

Europe's Growing Muslim Population. (2017, November 29). Washington: Pew Research Centre. Retrieved from pewforum.org.

Fallaci, O. (2006). *The force of reason*. New York: Rizzoli International Publications.

Fekete, Liz. (2012). The Muslim conspiracy theory and the Oslo massacre. *Race & Class, 53*(3), 30–47.

Finkielkraut, A. (2017). Le grand déménagement du monde. *France culture*. Retrieved from franceculture.fr.

Geller, P. (2010, May 15). The 911 imam. Atlas Shrugs blog. Retrieved from from pamelageller.com.

Gray, M. (2010). *Conspiracy theories in the Arab world: Sources and politics*. Abingdon-on-Thames: Routledge.

Hagelund, A. (2003). A matter of decency? The Progress Party in Norwegian immigration politics. *Journal of Ethnic and Migration Studies, 29*(1), 47–65.

Hellstrom, A. (2016). *Trust us: Reproducing the nation and the Scandinavian nationalist populist parties*. Oxford: Berghahn Books.

Huntington, S. (1993). The clash of civilizations? *Foreign Affairs, 72*(3), 14–33.

Huntington, S. (1996). *The clash of civilizations and the remaking of world order*. New York: Simon & Schuster.

Islamin yhdistäminen pedofiliaan toi Halla-aholle sakot myös hovilta. (2010, February 11). Helsinki: Mtv.fi.

Jespersen, K, Pittelkow, R., & Ahl, Nils. (2008). *Islamists and Naivists—An indictment*. Jerusalem: Jerusalem Centre for Public Affairs.

Jupskås, A. R. (2013). The Progress Party: A farily integrated part of the Norwegian party system. In Grabow & Hartleb (Eds.), *Expoising the demagogues: Right-wing and national populist parties in Europe*. Berlin: Konrad Adenauer Stiftung.

Jupskås, A. R. (2015). *The persistence of populism. The Norwegian Progress Party 1973–2009*. Faculty of Social Sciences, University of Oslo, no. 527.

Kessler, G. (2015, November 22). Trump's outrageous claim that "thousands" of New Jersey Muslims celebrated the 9/11 attacks. *Washington Post*. Washington.

Kinnvall, C., & Nesbitt-Larking, P. (2010). The political psychology of (de)securitization: Place-making strategies in Denmark, Sweden, and Canada. *Environment and Planning D: Society and Space, 28*(6), 1051–1070.

Klein, A. (2013). The end of solidarity? On the development of right-wing populist parties in Denmark and Sweden. In Garbow & Hartleb (Eds.), *Expoising the demagogues: Right-wing and national populist parties in Europe*. Berlin: Konrad Adenauer Stiftung.

Listhaug, S. (2018, March 14). *Facebook post*. Retrieved from facebook.com.

Lewis, B. (1990, September). The roots of Muslim rage. *The Atlantic*. Boston. Retrieved from theatlantic.com.

Majority say congressional hearings on alleged extremism in American Muslim community 'good idea.' (2011, February 16). Washington: Public Religion Research Institute. Retrieved from publicreligion.org.

Massie, A. (2016, June 16). A day of infamy. *The Spectator*. London. Retrieved from blogs.spectator.co.uk.

Meeting between Swedish and Norwegian ministers scrapped following "no-go zone" claims. (2017, August 29). *The Local*. Stockholm. Retrieved from thelocal.no.

Milne, R. (2017, August 30). Norway minister sparks war of words with Sweden over immigration. *The Financial Times*. London. Retrieved from ft.com.

Mouritsen, P., & Olsen, T. V. (2013). Denmark between liberalism and nationalism. *Ethnic and Racial Studies, 36*(4), 691–710.

Mudde, C. (2016). *On extremism and democracy in Europe*. Abingdon-on-Thames: Routledge.

Pettersen, S. V., & Østby, L. (2014). *Immigrants in Norway, Sweden and Denmark*. Oslo: Statistisk Sentralbyra. Retrieved from ssb.no.

Police to Investigate Helsinki City Council Member's Blog. (2008, December 12). Helsinki: Yle Uutiset. Retrieved from yle.fi/uutiset.

Potok, M. (2017). The year in hate and extremism. *Intelligence Report Magazine*. Montgomery: Southern Poverty Law Center. Retrieved from splcenter.org.

Potok, M., & Terry, D. (2015). *10 right-wing conspiracy theories that have slowly invaded American politics*. Salon. Retrieved from salon.com.

Pratt, D., & Woodlock, R. (2017). Introduction: Understanding Islamophobia. In Pratt &Wodlock (Eds.), *Fear of Muslims: International perspectives on Islamophobia*. Cham: Springer.

Raspail, J. (1994 [1974]). *The camp of the saints*. Petoskey: Social Contract Press.

Rosenberg, Y. (2017, August 14). "Jews will not replace us": Why white supremacists go after Jews. *Washington Post*. Washington.

Rosendahl, J., & Forsell, T. (2016, January 13). *Anti-immigrant "soldiers of odin" raise concern in Finland*. Reuters. Retrieved from reuters.com.

Rydgren, J. (2007). The sociology of the radical right. *Annual Review of Sociology, 33*, 241–262.

Rydgren, J. (2010). Radical right-wing populism in Denmark and Sweden: Explaining party system change and stability. *SAIS Review of International Affairs, 30*(1), 57–71.

Sæland, I. (2016, 02). *Facebook post*. Retrieved from facebook.com.

Schleifer, T. (2016, October 3). Donald Trump: "I think Islam hates us". Atlanta. Cnn.com.

SD-ledamote polisanmäld efter tal om muslimer. (2017, 27 November). Stockholm. Aftonbladet.se.

Serwer, A. (2011, May 18). Debunking sharia panic, ACLU edition. *The American Prospect*. Washington. Retrieved from prospect.org.

Sommer, N., & Aagaard, S. (2003). *Succes: Historien om Pia Kjærsgaard*. Copenhagen: Lindhardt & Ringhof.

Spencer, R. (2008). *Stealth jihad: How radical Islam is subverting America without guns or bombs*. Washington, DC: Regnery Publishing.

Stainforth, T. (2009). The Danish paradox: Intolerance in the land of perpetual compromise. *Review of European and Russian Affairs, 5*(1), 83–106.

Strickland, P. (2017, August 13). *Unite the right: White supremacists rally in Virginia*. Doha. Aljazeera.com.

Symons, E. K. (2017, 23. March). *Steve Bannon loves France*. Brussels. Politico. eu.

Walters, J. (2015, December 10). Trump ignores UK critics and claims country has "a massive Muslim problem". *The Guardian*. London.

Weaver, M., & Jacobs, B. (2017, November 29). Trump retweets British far-right leader's anti-Muslim videos. *The Guardian*. London.

Widfeldt, A. (2015). *Extreme right parties in Scandinavia*. Abingdon-on-Thames: Routledge.

Wilders, G. (2017, August 5). *Twitter post*. Retrieved from twitter.com.

Winneker, C. (2015, July 27). *Finnish politician declares war on "multiculturalism"*. Brussels. Politico.eu.

Wren, K. (2001). Cultural racism: Something rotten in the state of Denmark? *Social & Cultural Geography, 2*(2), 141–162.

Wright, S. (2017). Reproducing fear: Islamophobia in the United States. In Pratt & Wodlock (Eds.), *Fear of Muslims: International perspectives on Islamophobia*. Cham: Springer.

7

Transmission and Fake News

In a shady room on top of a local sports hall in the small rustic town of Veles, overlooking the Vardar river right in the centre of Macedonia, a group of juveniles were in early 2016, gathered around their laptops, fabricating bogus news stories for the US elections. Each of them could expect to make thousands of Euros a month, writing, for example, of the Pope endorsing Donald Trump for US President, that Democrat candidate Hillary Clinton had been indicted for crime—or reporting even much more far-fetched tales, such as her being the Antichrist.

Many of these teenagers were students of Mirko Ceselkoski, a notorious fake news legend of the formerly industrial town (Soares 2017). For over a decade, he had run several websites aimed mainly at American readers, earning a small fortune from, for example, the Google ads system. Initially, he offered his readers dubious health tips before turning to concocted political news. His young followers in the deprived Macedonian town of only fifty-five thousand inhabitants, stumbled, almost by accident, upon the lucrative business of fabricating mainly pro-Trump stories during the US presidential election.

Writer Samantha Subramanian (2017) interviewed one of the young fake news barons of Veles, who she named Boris in her story.

© The Author(s) 2018
E. Bergmann, *Conspiracy & Populism*, https://doi.org/10.1007/978-3-319-90359-0_7

Not being a proficient English writer himself, Boris describes in the interview how he plagiarised material from many alt-right and neo-Nazi websites in the US and posted them on his own sites. The only difference was that his sites were stripped of the neo-Nazi and alt-right symbols, which usually were splattered all over the websites he took the text from, and instead designed them to look like real news outlets. For example, to give it credibility, one site was hosted on the domain NewYorkTimesPolitics.com and resembled the genuine *New York Times* newspaper website. Boris would then share his posts on social media, for example, on the many Facebook groups covering US politics. From there, his fabricated stories spread to millions around the USA and, indeed, around the world. In a span of merely three months before the November 2016 US presidential elections, Boris earned almost $16,000 from his pro-Trump websites (Subramanian 2017).

The above-mentioned clickbait king of Veles, Mirko Ceselkoski, explains how the fake news industry took off amongst unemployed youngsters in the underprivileged town. 'It spread like fire', he said (Soares 2017). He estimated that around a hundred of his pupils were operating political news sites aimed at American readership. The teenagers of Veles approached their task impartially; they had no interest in US politics and couldn't care less who won the election. Across the Atlantic, however, these sorts of stories were firing up many people in the election debate.

The fake news factories interfering in the 2016 US election were, though, not all just bottom up, such as the one in Veles. Profiling company Cambridge Analytica has for instance been accused of exploiting personal data harvested from social media without permission to target voters dishonestly (Rosenberg et al. 2018). Influential Russians, with ties to the Kremlin, have also been accused of operating troll farms, for specific political gain. In 2018, the office of the US Special Prosecutor, Robert Mueller, for example, issued an indictment before a district court in Washington, DC, accusing 13 Russian nationals and three Russian companies—including a notorious troll factory' in St. Petersburg, called Internet Research Agency (IRA)—of a conspiracy. The indictment stated that IRA had conspired to 'defraud the United States by impairing, obstructing, and defeating the lawful functions of the government through fraud and deceit for the purpose of interfering with the US political and electoral processes, including the presidential election of 2016.'

The indictment maintained that the Russian computer bot farm invested large amounts of money to interfere in the US political system prior to the 2016 presidential election. The indictment insisted that via these troll factories they had, from 2014, spread pro-Donald Trump propaganda and fake news on social media platforms, such as Facebook and Twitter. The US investigation concluded that the primary source of funding for the operation had come from one Yevgeny Prigozhin, a Russian oligarch and close ally of President Vladimir Putin.

Whichever their origin, CTs, disguised as news, were since 2016, blazing like a snowstorm across the political scene on both sides of the Atlantic. In this chapter, I turn to discussing how populist political CTs are transmitted. A recent decline in trust of the mainstream media and increased importance of online media has proved to be a fertile ground for the spread of CTs. A specific focus here will, thus, be on the spread of populist CTs through fake news on the Internet, primarily on social media. First, however, I turn to framing the phenomena.

Framing Fake News

Fake news is the deliberate publication of fictitious communication, often spread for a political purpose. As established in previous chapters, CTs and fabricated news stories have been around for a long time. Spreading lies to demonise one's opponent has been an ongoing tactic for centuries—indeed, that is right out of Machiavelli's (1550) playbook. Oral transmissions, folklore, urban legends and rumours have always been floating around in human societies. Fake news, as such, is therefore nothing new. Throughout the twentieth century, for example, fake news was frequently spread via mainstream media. And often times, tales have been simmering in subcultures and rising to the surface only when the timing is ripe.

In his book, *How Mumbo-Jumbo Conquered the World*, Francis Wheen (2005), argues that reason is on the retreat in contemporary political discourse, that instead, 'cults, quacks, gurus, irrational panics, moral confusion and an epidemic of mumbo-jumbo' characterizes our era. Ween maintains that the values of the Enlightenment—the insistence on intellectual autonomy, commitment to free inquiry and dismissal of bigotry and persecution—are fast being abandoned.

In the last few decades, network television and especially the emergence of the 24-hour news broadcasts have proved to be fertile in transmitting CTs and fake news. In fact, as Rydgren (2007), for example, argues, the media has been an important enabling factor in the rise of populist parties in the West. Sindre Bangstad (2017) insists that the increasingly polarized nature of modern media, 'is rather favourable to the communication styles and formats of populist/radical right-wingers, which thrive on presenting political issues in starkly polarised and simplified manners.'

I have already (Chapter 5) mentioned the importance of television news in Russia for transmitting CTs upheld by the Kremlin. The large broadcasting outlets in the West have as well been keen on, for example, featuring conspiratorial documentaries, often without dismissing them as groundless. Jovan Byford (2011), for instance, notes how even CNN in the US broadcasted the agenda of the so-called *Birther* movement.

In the world of political radio and TV talk shows, prejudices often prevail over facts. Byford discusses how it is an inherent feature of cable television networks specialising in historical documentaries, such as the History Channel and Discovery Channel, that 'conspiratorial and non-conspiratorial interpretations are presented as equally reasonable positions in a legitimate debate.' He concludes that contributors to these programs tend to be presented equally as experts 'be they scholars, engineers, forensic experts, trained historians, amateur enthusiasts, ufologists or conspiracy buffs.'

The recent emergence of online and social media might, thus, not have altered the inner nature of fake news, but they have surely completely transformed their transmission. These modern mediums have, over a very short span of time, provided the public with unprecedented and unhindered access to a wide range of information. The Internet soon became the principle instrument of spreading CTs. Together with the 24-hour rolling television news, the combination of the two provided the vehicle for faster take-off than before. One side effect of this evolution has, thus, proved to be easier and more powerful transmission of CTs. CTs have not only increased in numbers, but also spread further and become larger in scope than before. As result, fake news has impacted political discussion in recent years to the extent that debates in democratic elections have increasingly come to revolve round fabricated stories cropping up online.

In the UK Brexit referendum debate, one such story, for example, insisted that the notorious Bilderberg group was, in secret, plotting to prevent Britain from leaving the EU. As discussed in Chapter 2, CTs around the Bilderberg group are widespread, for instance, asserting that it is, in effect, a shadow world government; that it 'pulls the strings with which national governments dance.' Amongst those promoting the story during the Brexit debate was UKIP MEP, Gerard Batten, who believed that the EU was conceived by Nazi Germany (Stone 2016).

For the purpose of this book, fake news of contemporary times can be framed, here, as the deliberate publication of fabricated tales spread mainly online for personal, political or financial gain. This, obviously, is related to political propaganda, i.e., in fabricating stories for the purpose of influencing people's opinion.

Social Media and the Post-truth Era

Social media has emerged as online publics. The gate keeping role of the mainstream media of the twentieth century is largely gone. Proliferation of online media in recent years has been such that the world was flooded with indiscriminate information, in which people could not easily separate facts from fabrications. We are indeed living in times of unprecedented access to all kinds of information. And while that is surely democratic and empowering for ordinary people, we are also being exposed to much more unscrutinised information than ever before. This overflow of information can leave us incapable of interpreting it properly. In effect, thus, too much information can result in us absorbing no meaningful knowledge at all. And when everything is true, nothing is true—rendering all criticism against authorities as futile. This opens up a space for misinformation to thrive in the public sphere, leaving democratic societies vulnerable to manipulation.

This new environment led to a political culture emerging, which has been branded *Post-Truth* politics (*The Economist* 2016a). In this situation, where people also tend to get trapped within their own echo chamber, a discourse appealing to emotions started to grow stronger than factual reasoning. Contradictions were openly embraced and, as a result, it became easier to disconnect the public debate from established knowledge. In return, previously stigmatised knowledge—the kind of which was discussed in Chapter 3—was increasingly accepted, and facts became less important than personal beliefs. Here is how a conservative talk-show host in the US, Charlie Sykes, explained this change: 'We've basically eliminated any of the referees, the gatekeepers …There is nobody: you can't go to nobody and say: 'Look, here are the facts'' (cited in *the Economist* 2016b). In this vein, Yale Professor Timothy Snyder (2017) equates Post-Truth with Pre-Fascism.

Right-wing populists and conspiracy theorists united in opposition to the mainstream media, and against established knowledge, which they claimed was produced by the elite and eschewed in favour of the powerful. Many of these actors saw the established press as distorters and concealers of the truth, indeed as an inherited part of the very conspiracy system they were fighting against (Barkun 2013). Mainstream media was thus often the target of populist conspiracy theorists. In part, this is due to the tendency of people, in general, to believe that the media has a greater effect on others than on oneself (Bartlett and Miller 2010).

For many extreme and peripheral groups, the Internet was a sheer godsend, as it provided them with the means of bypassing the former gate-keeping role of the mainstream media. Neo-Nazis and Islamist terrorists alike utilised social media to get their messages across. For example, J. M. Berger (2016) found that in the four years from 2012 to 2016, American white nationalist movements increased their following six fold on Twitter. Their most common theme of discussion on the platform was the CT of *white genocide*. Perhaps unsurprisingly, the study found that followers of white nationalists on Twitter in the USA predominantly supported Donald Trump for president. Apart from white genocide, they referred to him more often in 2016 than to any other topic. The most tweeted video on YouTube by white nationalists in America was a documentary titled *Adolf Hitler: The Greatest*

Story Never Told. The collection of footage insists that Hitler was not the monster he is portrayed as being in the mainstream media, and by established knowledge, but that he, in fact, was a brave fighter against the world's most evil forces: Zionist bankers and economic elite (Berger 2016).

With diminished gate-keeping capabilities of the mainstream media it, thus, becomes ever more difficult for people to distinguish between factual stories and fictitious news often spread via unscrupulous websites, as both can be presented in the same guise. And once a false story of a conspiracy takes hold, it can proof difficult to uproot (Douglas et al. 2017).

Tellingly for this turn, authoritative governments such as in China, thus, have gradually moved away from censoring content on the Internet. Instead, they increasingly flood the wires and networks with distracting information. This is similar to the tactics of, for example, Turkey and Russia. Turkish writer Zeynep Tufekci (2016) of the University of North Carolina maintained that information glut, indeed, was the new censorship. 'Once, censorship worked by blocking crucial pieces of information. In this era of information overload, censorship works by drowning us in too much undifferentiated information, crippling our ability to focus.'

Pizza-Gate and the USA

In March 2016, many people's newsfeed on Facebook and Twitter were suddenly filled with stories indicating that Hillary Clinton and other Democrats were secretly running a paedophile ring out of a pizza parlour in Washington, DC. The gobsmacking revelations were tagged *pizza-gate*. The reporting entailed that the exposé was found in leaked e-mails of Clinton's campaign chairman, John Podesta, published by *WikiLeaks*. The e-mails were reported to contain coded message about human trafficking and the paedophile operation. By the November presidential election, more than a million tweets had been sent with the hashtag #pizzagate (Douglas et al. 2017). The coming months saw an avalanche of bogus stories cropping up all over the Internet.

The consequences of these sorts of concocted stories—and those coming out of the Macedonian town of Veles, discussed at the beginning of this chapter—came in various versions. Here is one example: On 4 December 2016, one Edgar Welch stormed into the Comet Ping Pong pizza parlour in Washington, DC on a mission to rescue abused children he thought were being kept there. Armed with an assault rifle, he had travelled from North Carolina to the restaurant, to break up the paedophile kidnapping ring that he had read about online. After quite a commotion and a couple of shots fired, Welch was finally faced with the fact that Hillary Clinton and her aides were not tormenting kidnapped children there. It was just a pizza joint. Only after the incident, did Welch come to realise that the data he obtained online about the alleged evil operation was inaccurate. Afterwards, he explained to an interviewer, that 'the intel on this wasn't 100 percent' (cited in Hannon and Hannon 2016). In 2017, Welch was sentenced to four years in prison. He, the pizza joint, Hillary Clinton, and indeed US voters, all fell victim to a fabricated CT spread as news online.

Throughout this book, many similar fake news stories from the US have been discussed. One, for instance, insisted that Democrats wanted to impose Islamic Sharia law in Florida. On the opposite side of the political spectrum, a false story wrongly indicated that thousands of Donald Trump supporters were chanting at a rally in Manhattan, 'We hate Muslims, we hate blacks, we want our great country back' (Qiu 2016).

It is telling for the post-truth times we are living in, that after having been accused of promoting fake-news stories, similar to those that have been discussed here, Donald Trump turned the allegation on its head and started systematically to brand the mainstream media outlets of spreading fake news. Steve Coll (2017), of the magazine *The New Yorker*, finds that Trump's definition of fake news seems, most generally, simply to be 'credible reporting that he doesn't like.'

Although fake news might recently have spread further in the USA than in most places, it was also prevalent in Europe, for example, in the Brexit debate in the UK, as was discussed in the two preceding chapters. Next, I turn to addressing the fake news factory of the Kremlin in Russia.

Russia's Misinformation Tactics

Angela Merkel is the secret daughter of Adolf Hitler and the EU is preparing to ban snowmen. As snowmen are all white, it is, thus, racist to build them. Anyone forming a white human from snow has also to include yellow and black versions, otherwise they will be fined €5000 by the EU for racism. Furthermore, Sweden is on the verge of civil war and animal prostitution was legalized in Denmark. These are only few of the fabricated news stories that the East StratCom group—a task force set up by the EU mapping fake news—detected in the state media in Russia in 2017 alone (see on euvsdisinfo.eu). In total, the group identified 1310 fake news stories coming out of Russia that year.

While averring that the mainstream media was silencing this grim fact, one of these fabricated stories insisted that due to immigration, rapes in Sweden had in only two years, between 2015 and 2017, increased by a thousand percent (AC24 2017). Furthermore, it was asserted that the liberal and social democratic leaders in Europe were celebrating even this darker side of migration. One story stated that the foreign minister of Sweden, Margot Wallström, was contemplating a proposition of sterilising all white men in Sweden, to prevent them from breeding further. Incidentally, that is not true and reported rapes in Sweden in 2017 were up by only 1.4 percent since 2015.

As discussed in Chapter 5, Russia has become increasingly conspiratorial. In these stories, often produced and promoted by the state, the West was systematically treated as the ultimate *other*, who was hostile and seeking to prevent Russia from flourishing. One of the reports detected by the East StratCom group (2017), insisted that Germany was a deteriorating but aggressive state in support of Nazis in Ukraine. According to the story, Germany was, via a large scale Nato build-up in the Baltics, planning to invade St. Petersburg. Authorities in Berlin were also accused of a plot which would turn Europe into a German colony (hidfo.ru 2017).

Amongst the main themes identified in these stories was a US plot of occupying Europe. One of these stories reported that the US Air Force had already bombed Lithuania in 2017. Another indicated that French President, Emmanuel Macron, was an agent of the US Department of the Treasury. The report said that he was backed by homosexual lobby-ists and also by the wealthy Rothschild family.

One example of conspiratorial diversion tactics of the Russian state came in the wake of the assassination attempt of a former Russian coun-ter-spy in the UK, Sergei Skripal, who previously had worked for British authorities. The Russian state, which viewed Skripal as being a traitor, stood accused of having poisoned him on British soil. While deny-ing any involvement, Russian permanent secretary to the UN, Vasily Nebenzya, suggested that the UK government was itself behind the incident, in an act of 'black PR,' designed to 'tarnish Russia' (Oliphant 2018)—Russian officials maintained that the poison was produced in Britain, and even suggested that the UK was, with the plot, merely try-ing to get out of the 2018 world football championship in Moscow.

In these tales, discussed above, Russia was generally portrayed as the innocent actor under siege by a violent foreign aggressor, the evil West. The story of the Punk band, Pussy Riot, which I turn to discussing next, is illustrative of how the state was, via fabricated news stories, able to dismiss domestic dissidents as external threats emanating from the West.

Pussy Riot

In February 2012, five young women attempted to perform what they called punk-prayer in the Cathedral of Christ the Saviour in Moscow. The title of their song was telling for their aim: *Mother of God, Drive Putin Away*. Ahead of the presidential elections in the following month, the female punk band Pussy Riot became the leading voice of much larger ongoing protests against Vladimir Putin's regime. At first, the young women had been dismissed as some sorts of hooligans but soon after the stunt in the Moscow cathedral, they were treated by authori-ties as perhaps enemy number one of the Russian nation. Three of them were arrested and sentenced to two years in prison. Since then, several members of band have faced repeated arrests and incarcerations.

Russian authorities launched an aggressive media campaign, in which the protestors were, in a series of television reports, depicted as being part of a Western led plan to undermine Russian statehood and prevent Russia from fulfilling its full potential at home and in the world (Yablokov 2014). Members of Pussy Riot and other domestic dissidents were, in these invented stories, linked to foreign intelligence agencies. They were branded traitors of the people, posing a threat of splitting the Russian nation apart.

Their criticism of the regime and the social unrest that had followed in the wake of the December 2011 parliamentary election in Russia were all dismissed by the Kremlin as mere undermining tactics of Western forces, who had the aim of weakening Russia. Similarly, the Kremlin responded to the February 2012 protests by launching a massive media campaign where members of Pussy riot and other protesters were depicted as agents of Western forces, who were aiming to destabilise, and, indeed, to emasculate Russia.

Ilya Yablokov (2014) has illustrated how the Russian regime aggressively promoted a discursive division of *Us* and *Them*. In doing so, authorities could treat the protestors as foreign infiltrators who were undermining an otherwise united Russian nation. By depicting them as foreign conspirators, Russian authorities were able to portray members of the punk band and other dissenting actors as posing a major threat to Russian statehood. They were, for example, dismissed as immoral deviants, sexual perverts, witches, blasphemers and provocateurs who were supported by the West, and utterly alien to the ordinary Russian people (Yablokov 2014). Via media reporting, the young women of Pussy Riot were discursively turned into *others*, and, thus, made distinct from the Russian nation.

The discourse that followed in the domestic media was highly conspiratorial. Almost all dissenting voices were domestically portrayed as part of the overall Western conspiracy of ruining Russia. Many within the Russian government, for instance, argued that Pussy Riot was a Western revenge plot, sent to demoralise the Russian nation, and to demonize the Russian government for standing up to Washington's intention to destroy Syria. In this vein, the regime was able to assert that they were faced with disruptive forces that threatened the very unity of Russian society. In the media campaign, the protesters were, thus, depicted as being a conspiring minority within the nation, perhaps much like a cancer that needed to be uprooted.

Furthermore, all criticism from abroad of the harsh treatment of the young women could be scorned as part of the external plot. Indeed, critical reporting from abroad were taken as proof of the Western led conspiracy.

References

Art of the lie. (2016a, September 10). London. Economist.com.

Yes, I'd lie to you. (2016b, October 9). London. Economist.com.

Bangstad, S. (2017). Norwegian right-wing discourses: Extremism post-Utøya. In Pratt & Wodlock (Eds.), Fear of Muslims international perspectives on Islamophobia. Cham: Springer.

Barkun, M. (2013). *A culture of conspiracy: Apocalyptic visions in contemporary America*. Berkeley: University of California Press.

Bartlett, J., & Miller, C. (2010). *The power of unreason: Conspiracy theories, extremism and counter-terrorism*. London: Demos. Retrieved from western-voice.net.

Berger, J. M. (2016). *Nazis vs. ISIS on Twitter: A comparative study of white nationalist and ISIS online social media networks*. Washington: George Washington University Program on Extremism Report. Retrieved from cchs.gwu.edu.

Byford, J. (2011). *Conspiracy theories: A critical introduction*. Basingstoke: Palgrave Macmillan.

Byla to obrovská legrace! Uvedl migrant, který společně s devatenácti parťáky brutálně znásilnil třicetiletou ženu ve Švédsku. (2017, December 9). *Ac24. cz*. Prague.

Coll, S. (2017, December 3). Donald Trump's "fake news" tactics. *The New Yorker*. New York.

Douglas, K., Ang, C. S., & Deravi, F. (2017). Reclaiming the truth. *Psychologist, 30*, 36–40.

Hannon, E., & Hannon, E. (2016, December 7). Comet Pizzeria Gunman says "the intel on this wasn't 100 percent" in first interview. New York. *Slate.com*.

Indictment in the United States District Court for the District of Columbia. Criminal No (18 U.S.C. §§ 2, 371, 1349, 1028A). Retrieved from justice.gov.

Machiavelli, N. (1550). *The prince*.

Német gyarmat lenne az Európai Egyesült Államok. (2017, December 14). *Hidfo.ru.* Moscow.

Nuclear bombs over Lithuania? (2017, June 23). Brussels: EU vs Disinfo [European External Action Service, East Stratcom Task Force]. Retrieved from euvsdisinfo.eu.

Oliphant, R. (2018, March 16). Putin aid in Cold War warning as UK linkened to 'hapless inspector.' *Independent.ie.* Dublin.

Qiu, L. (2016, 9 November). *No evidence to support rumors of 'We hate Muslims' chant at Trump victory rally.* Washington: Politifact.com.

Rosenberg, M., Confessore, N., & Cadwalladr, C. (2018, 17 March). *How Trump Consultants Exploited the Facebook Data of Millons.* New York: The New York Times.

Rydgren, J. (2007). The sociology of the radical right. *Annual Review of Sociology, 33,* 241–262.

Snyder, T. (2017). *On tyranny: Twenty lessons from the twentieth century.* New York: Tim Duggan Books.

Soares, I. (2017). The fake news machine: Inside a town gearing up for 2020. *Cnn.com.* Atlanta.

Stone, J. (2016, May 16). Nazis created 'basic plan' for European Union, Ukip MEP Gerard Batten says. *Independent.co.uk.* London.

Subramanian, S. (2017, Summer). The Macedonian teens who mastered fake news. *Wired.* New York. Retrieved from wired.com.

Tufekci, Z. (2016, November 4). WikiLeaks isn't whistleblowing. *The New York Times.* New York.

What didn't happen in 2017? (2017, December 21). Brussels: EU vs Disinfo [European External Action Service East Stratcom Task Force]. Retrieved from euvsdisinfo.eu.

Wheen, F. (2005). *How Mumbo-Jumbo conquered the world: A short history of modern delusions.* Nashville: Public Affairs.

Yablokov, I. (2014). Pussy Riot as agent provocateur: Conspiracy theories and the media construction of nation in Putin's Russia. *Nationalities Papers, 42*(4), 622–636.

8

Conclusions: The Politics of Misinformation

Norwegian terrorist, Anders Behring Breivik, discussed at the beginning of this book was a believer in the so-called *Eurabia* conspiracy theory (CT). He was convinced that domestic traitors were conspiring to turn Norway—and, indeed, most of Europe—into an Islamic society. Similar to what has often, for instance, been the case within Muslim jihad environments, Breivik was radicalised via online networks, where multiculturalism was vilified, and violence was glorified. He saw himself as a Christian knight, fighting against both external evil and domestic traitors. His targets were those he called cultural Marxists within the Norwegian Labour Party, who he accused of being responsible for ruining his country's Nordic heritage. In 2011, he massacred 77 of them.

Breivik was a lone wolf attacker, still, he falls into a group of several like-minded violent actors. Others of a related mind, who have been discussed in this book, include, for instance, Thomas Mair in the UK. On similar ideological grounds, Mair murdered Labour Party Member of Parliament, Joe Cox, during the Brexit campaign in 2016. He also saw himself as a defender of Christian Europe, fighting for the ordinary people against white traitors of their own people, the left-wing liberals he thought were responsible for ruining the Western world.

© The Author(s) 2018
E. Bergmann, *Conspiracy & Populism*, https://doi.org/10.1007/978-3-319-90359-0_8

A third example is, for instance, found in the belief system which drove Timothy McVeigh to blow up the US federal building in Oklahoma in 1995. McVeigh belonged to anti-government survivalist militias. He was convinced that the US government was waging a war on the public and was plotting to instate authoritarian dictatorship. Just like Breivik and Mair, McVeigh also saw himself as protector of the people against their malignant government.

These sorts of domestic terrorists were surely out on the furthest fringes, and non-violent right-wing populists cannot be held directly responsible for their actions. However, although these horrible violent actions were surely the exception, they still show the violent effects that far-right conspiracy theorists can have on unstable recipients of their messages. These acts of terror, thus, cannot be understood without reference to the ideologies which the perpetrators claimed legitimized their actions.

In recent years, Western societies have seen rising support for varieties of nationalist populist political parties. Many of them have tapped into similar political and philosophical sources that framed the thinking of Breivik, Mair, McVeigh and others of a like mind. Ironically, their extremism is, however, much more comparable to violent radical-left terror groups in Europe in the 1970s, like the Red Army Faction in Germany, and, indeed, contemporary Islamist terrorists, such as al-Qaida and Isis. The violent-left tapped into ordinary socialist literature and Islamist terrorists have based their horrific deeds on even mainstream religious texts.

One of Breivik's main political heroes was Dutch far-right leader Geert Wilders, mentioned earlier in this book, who Breivik cited 30 times in his lengthy and rampant manifesto. In other words, much of the content in Breivik's hate speech was not very novel in the milieu of right-wing extremists. Rather, only his actions were so exceptional.

Conspiracy theories are of various kinds, ranging from, for instance, suspicions around isolated incidents, such as single assassinations, to complex discursive constructions, like those built by John Todd, discussed earlier in this book, who maintained that a modern version of the Illuminati, together with, for example, the Rothschild family, were plotting to take over control in the world. Another magnificent conspiratorial conglomerate was constructed by British author,

David Icke. He insisted that the world was already controlled by a vast network of secret societies—the *Brotherhood*—a Global Elite, which was sitting on top of a vast world dominating pyramid, in which the Illuminati was one of many components. In later versions, Icke insisted that the Brotherhood, in turn, was itself controlled by extra-terrestrial reptiles.

Classical CTs of far-right and neo-Nazi groups have, for example, revolved around ideas of a communist New World Order being plotted against the Christian white community. Many of these have gained a wide following, as has been discussed here. The plotters were often seen to be a mixture of liberals, Marxists, homosexuals, feminists and others of a similar sort who had taken control of both governments and media.

The radical-right has also tapped into some of the more far-fetched creations, such as into New Ages theories, tales of UFOs, prophesies like that of Nostradamus, and notions of an Illuminati-like New World Order. Juxtapositioning these with anti-government theories of the far-right has led to many novel compositions of innovative hybrid theories.

As has been documented here, most extremist groups firmly apply CTs in their discourse. For instance, most anti-government patriot movements in the US steadfastly believed that the government was secretly planning to impose martial law and confiscate all privately held guns. Another category revolved around various versions of deep-state theories.

Recently, CTs have increasingly come to revolve around issues having more direct consequences on contemporary socio-political developments, such as European integration and globalization. In these CTs, elite actors within the global system, such as the Bilderberg group, were suspected of plotting against the people across borders.

A remarkably persistent CT of the radical-right has revolved around suspicions of a band of Jews controlling world governments, the theory of a Zionist Occupied Government. Although most of these groups have recently turned to suspecting Muslims of malignant intentions in the West, anti-Semitism was still a surprisingly central theme in most of them. This, for instance, became evident in the alt-right and white supremacist's riots in Charlottesville in Virginia in the US in 2017, where ideas of a white genocide were also still afloat.

Conspiracy theories seem to fulfil a human need of making sense of an otherwise chaotic existence. They denounce official accounts of events and instead view the world as being designed by evil elites, who, in secret, are systematically plotting to advance their own interests, while harming the innocent and unknowing ordinary people. Usually, these are discursive creations where the conspiracy theorist is placed as a heroic whistle-blower, standing alone between the pure public he is protecting and the evil actor.

In essence, CTs are unverifiable truths. Belief in a CT, thus, becomes rather a matter of faith than proof. These are closed explanatory systems of counter-truths that cannot be verified. Conspiracy theories always insist on both secrecy and agency. The brave truth-teller strives to unravel secret evil deeds of identifiable agents, revealing an active deception of the powerful conspirator.

Conspiracy theories are not necessarily always wrong. Indeed, many examples exist of CTs later proven right, as has been discussed here. Still, CTs present an alternative narrative to existing knowledge. In other words, we are dealing with implausible accounts of events; not with credible rival explanations. Instead, CTs are understood here as unprovable counter cultural claims that contradict conventional accounts of events, irrespective of the evidence.

Alternative critical accounts of, for example, the capitalist system being rigged against the ordinary man is, thus, not necessarily a CT, if it lacks a secret agency of identifiable group of conspirators. However, as has been discussed here, when maintaining that the malignant order is controlled by, for instance, the Bilderberg group, that moves the explanation within the parameters of a CT. Thus, what sets CTs apart from critical theory is the insistence on agency, and on secret intention. The malevolent system must be set up by the design of the plotters.

Alongside the increased spread of CTs, populist political parties are also surging in the West. And just like CTs, populism can also be viewed as a discursive style in its own right. As has been discussed here, it can even be seen as a specific kind of conspiratorialism. Similar to CTs, who have often been dismissed as having delusional pathology, many have attempted to dismiss populists in the same way. Still, as has been mapped here, populists have recently gained far too much and widespread support for them all to be easily marginalized and dismissed as merely a paranoid deviation from normal politics.

Definitions of populism have been quite fleeting in the literature. Most often, though, populists attempt to mobilize the masses against the elite. In this book, the focus has primarily been on far-right nationalist populists, who in recent years, have found even mainstream support for their fight against migration and multiculturalism in the West. Polls have shown that authoritarian and anti-immigrant sentiments are no longer only isolated on the fringes; instead, key aspects of the populist radical-right are now shared with many of the mainstream.

In exploring common qualities of the broad church of right-wing nationalist populists, discussed here, the following frame applied in this book can be useful for understanding the phenomena. First of all, right-wing populists in Europe are nationalist, anti-immigrant, anti-elitist, anti-intellectual and Eurosceptic moralists who are economically protectionist, promoters of law and order, and foes to multicultural development on the continent. They speak to emotions rather than reason; they are nativists who distinguish between *us* and *them* and rely on strong charismatic leaders who advocate simple solutions to complex issues burdening the ordinary man.

Taken collectively, they put forth a threefold claim for support of the people: First, they discursively create an external threat to the nation; second, they accuse the domestic elite of betraying the people, often of even siding with the external forces; third, they position themselves as the only true defenders of the pure people they vow to protect against these malignant outsiders, that is, against those that they themselves have discursively created.

As has been established here, we have been living the times of the conspiratorial right-wing populists. Although each still being a separate phenomenon, CTs and populism share many attributes—such as not minding the existence of contradictions in their narrative. So, what is shared and where do the two depart?

One of the main identifying features of right-wing populism is found in its polarizing division between the people and the elite. The same is true with CTs. Both tropes divide between an innocent public and a malignant elite—countering the pure people and a corrupt elite, clearly distinguishing between the unknowing people and their conspirators who are in positions of power. In this shared *Mancherian* worldview, politics is cast as binary struggle between the people and the undeserving self-serving political class. Both strands, thus, offer the same binary scheme to understand events and a state of affairs, based on a similar polarised worldview, discursively creating an external threat to the inner group. This has been described as the shared duality of both populism and CTs.

Conspiracy theories have, in fact, been one of the most striking features in the discourse of populist political parties. In some ways, CTs are a form of populist protest, a form of radical populist discourse. As has been documented in this book, the populist far-right in the West increasingly identifies evil-doers in politics, who are seen to conspire against the ordinary public—for example, global elites who are secretly conspiring to create a totalitarian New World Order.

Populists tend to brand their opponents as elite; now often consisting of self-serving politicians, capitalists, journalists and academics, as well as functionaries of international institutions such as the EU. The dangerous *others*—that is, the enemies who the elite is preventing them from fighting—then tend to be foreign forces, migrants, mainly Muslims, and other minorities. In this discursive creation, CTs are firmly built into the populist message.

Many distinctions can still be found between the two phenomena. For example, when it comes to kinds of dualism. While populists tend to contrast the corrupt elite with the pure people, CTs tend to contrast conspirators with the unknowing people.

The relationship between populism and CTs can be quite ambiguous. For instance, one of the main features of populism is offering simple solutions to complex problems. Similarly, the simplicity of CTs—solving complex issues by pointing to a single grand plot—is, as well, one of the main appeals of CTs. However, CTs depart from populist analysis by offering incredibly detailed analysis of complex power relations. That is where populism enters conspiratorialism.

Another distinction is that populists have political aims, which is not a necessary ingredient in all CTs.

Studies have found that belief in CTs correlates highly with being susceptible to populist politics. Those that see the system as being stacked against them are far more likely to both believe in CTs and support populist political parties. They are likely to have less trust in society and be angry at authorities. Furthermore, both strands share anti-elitism and a mistrust of experts. Conspiracy theories and populism, thus, tend to complement each other.

One of the most prominent contemporary CTs of the populist-right discussed in this book is that of Eurabia. Warning that an influx of migrant Muslims to Europe will alter the face and fabric of the continent is, though, not necessarily a CT, not as such. However, when insisting that an identifiable group of plotters in the Middle East are covertly acting to take over Europe, then we have entered the conspiratorial world. And when adding to the mix, tales of domestic traitors collaborating with the external plotters—for instance, cultural Marxists, like both Anders Breivik and Thomas Mair insisted—then, a fully-fledged far-right populist conspiracy theory has been built.

In recent years, anti-Muslim sentiments have largely become legitimized in the West. Muslims are often cast as external invaders in a coordinated plot to conquer Europe. The development of this Eurabia theory in the Nordic countries, as discussed earlier in this book, is illustrative of how the tale travels. In only few decades the Nordics went from being open and emphasising tolerance of foreign cultures to unifying around increased restrictions on immigration. The nationalist populist parties in the region had all become nativist and exclusionary, distinguishing clearly between *Us* and *Them*. All vowed to stem immigration.

The Danish People's Party turned staunchly anti-immigrant, mainly anti-Muslim and squarely opposed Denmark becoming multicultural. Severely xenophobic factions also thrived within the Finns Party, aggressively fighting against Islamic influences. In Norway, the Progress Party likewise implied a foreign infiltration: that migrants were sucking blood from the welfare system at the expense of native Norwegians.

The Sweden Democrats played on fears of Sweden being overflowed with foreigners. They clearly distinguished between the native population, which they vowed to protect, and outsiders, which were often presented as an existential threat to the Swedish nation. The SD went as far as implying that the Social Democratic leadership was plotting to introducing Sharia laws in some parts of Sweden. Their local council member, Martin Strid, even indicated that Muslims were not fully human.

The literature on CTs has tended to focus on the marginalised and the powerless, the paranoid and delusional. However, as has been established here, populist CTs have also often been upheld by the powerful, for example, by authoritarian regimes to crush dissidents. Indeed, CTs remain the refuge of dictators and authoritarian leaders around the world. In the past century, we have seen democratic politics also becoming increasingly conspiratorial. Such examples include McCarthyism and the Red Scare in the US in the wake of the Second World War, the rhetoric on which right-wing populists in Europe like the *Front National* in France rose on three waves since the 1970s, and most recently, in the politics of state leaders, such as Hungarian President Viktor Orbán, US President Donald Trump and Russian President Vladimir Putin. These leaders have been found to uphold a rhetorical division of *Us* versus *Them* and all have taken their countries down a more authoritarian path. This trend turns conspiracy theorists away from the fringes and the underprivileged and has led to a process of mainstreaming the margins.

When upheld by the powerful, previously discredited CTs enter into a process of legitimatization and, thus, pose a threat to the liberal political system stemming from the very power centres themselves.

One of the defining features of populists—and arguably much of their appeal—is their willingness to dismiss the once universal values of liberal democracies: rule of law, diversity, openness, free cross border trade, human rights, free press, etc. Indeed, they tend to base their very claims to power precisely on a disrespect for established democratic norms—against the establishment they claim is manipulating the innocent public. This is where populism most clearly departs from mainstream parties and break away from the status quo—quite often by way of CTs, as has been explored here.

A process of the normalization of conspiratorial populist politics occurred when many mainstream parties in the West started to follow suit. This has turned into a process in the direction of eroding the once shared democratic norms of the West.

As has been established here, politicians and activists often deliberately apply CTs to spread fear and distrust in society. Of course, rumours, lies and rhetorical manipulations have been common tactics used by leaders throughout the centuries. Most recently, however, this has been done via fake news and by what can be understood as the politics of misinformation—which have been amplified after the gatekeeping role of the mainstream media was largely removed.

More generally, it can be concluded that the post-truth political environment has fuelled right-wing populist CTs and fake news and, in the process, has served to undermine trust in western societies.

Populist actors in politics often position themselves as the true defenders of the people, heroically standing against an external threat. Simultaneously, they point a finger at others in the domestic elite who they accuse of having betrayed the public. This is the process of identifying enemies of the people. The scapegoats are always outsiders—an external evil and/or a corrupt elite—never those who belong to the in-group.

This has proved to be a very powerful rhetorical construction. In demonising *the other*, who the inner group defines itself against, the conspiratorial populist also turns to delegitimizing domestic voices of dissent, casting them as part of the conspiracy and enabling the external threat. One feature of this process is in casting opponents as enemies of the people, rather than merely being political adversaries. This has moved the political rhetoric towards a more militant direction than before. A wedge of distrust is, thus, cast between different groups in society.

This, for example, occurs by a process of de-humanization, as was the case with the Jews in Nazi Germany, which, for example, referred to Jewish people as 'rats' and 'fungus,' and gradually stripped them of basic human rights.

Though perhaps on a more modest scale, this was still the same tactic applied by, for example, Marine Le Pen in France when referring to Raspail's novel discussed in Chapter 6. She insisted that Europe was being invaded by hordes of 'stinking' dark-skinned migrants and 'rat people' flowing in a 'river of sperm.'

Another example is of the Sweden Democrat local council member, discussed above, who implied that Muslims were not fully human. A third example of a similar process of de-humanization of an out-group occurred in Norway, when Roma people had set up camp in Oslo. The camp suffered numerous attacks and they were described as 'rats,' and of being 'inhuman.'

The most horrible effects of this sort of politics can be seen in the cases of Anders Breivik, Thomas Mair, Timothy McVeigh and others of their kind discussed throughout in this book. After having externalised their victims as being part of outgroups subscribing to different values than theirs—effectively turning them into an *Other*—the killing becomes easier. The victims are stripped of their humanity.

Populist CTs can, thus, come to erode trust in society. They have been found to be a catalyst for radicalization and extremism. A direct linear relationship has, indeed, been found between extremism, in practise, and belief in CTs.

As has been established here, many conspiratorial far-right extremists have become convinced of their just cause: of defending their society against an external threat that society is facing, and against the domestic elite, which they believe has betrayed the public. In doing so, they tend to justify the violence as a necessary defence against external evil.

Index

© The Editor(s) (if applicable) and The Author(s) 2018
E. Bergmann, *Conspiracy & Populism*, https://doi.org/10.1007/978-3-319-90359-0